KENNY RICHEY
DEATH ROW SCOT

Author Tom Richey emigrated to America in 1985 and, like his older brother Kenny, also found trouble with the law. He has now spent twenty years in jail in the USA but his bond with his brother Kenny remains as strong as ever. He has played a key role in the fight to free Kenny Richey and has spent the last ten years meticulously researching the case and helping with the Kenny Richey Campaign. He, too, hopes to be free soon, having served his time for the crime he committed.

KENNY RICHEY

DEATH ROW SCOT

MY BROTHER KENNY'S FIGHT FOR JUSTICE

TOM RICHEY

FOREWORD BY
KENNY RICHEY

BLACK & WHITE PUBLISHING

First published 2005
by Black & White Publishing Ltd
99 Giles Street, Edinburgh, Scotland

ISBN 1 84502 064 2

British Library Cataloguing in Publication Data:
A catalogue record for this book is available
from the British Library.

Cover image of Electric Chair © Corbis

Printed and bound by Creative Print & Design

CONTENTS

ACKNOWLEDGEMENTS

I want to thank the following people for making this book possible: Sylvia Smith for providing my typewriter; Kelly Downs for being my beacon; Dad, for providing necessary materials; Mum, for delivering the manuscript; and my brother Kenny, for being my worst critic (may the Garden of Eden open its gates and allow you its tastiest fruits). I also want to thank Campbell Brown, Managing Director at Black & White Publishing, for making Scotland my land of opportunity.

T.R.

FOREWORD
BY
KENNY RICHEY

When my brother proposed writing a book about my case, I was sceptical for several reasons. Firstly, he had no experience of writing a book and, secondly, he was, himself, living in a concrete cell, isolated from the resources that are readily available to other writers. It sounded like such a monumental task for someone in his position and then, even if he accomplished writing the book, I had some doubts he'd be taken seriously by the publishing world. But Tom always did like a challenge and I suppose that's why we know about people like Sir Edmund Hillary – men who go forward in the face of adversity. This book was Tom's Everest and I'm grateful to him for conquering it.

I wouldn't wish what happened to me on anyone and I wanted my story to be told. In telling it, Tom has gone beyond my expectations. He has written a true and accurate account of my life leading up to my arrest, through my trial and during my years on death row. I didn't always make it easy for him. At times, I nit-picked, but he had the sense to give in to me when I was right and stand his ground when I was wrong. What he has created is a work that is fairly and objectively written.

I don't know what will be achieved by publishing my story. I hope it will contribute to change in Ohio State and other places where the judicial system is broken. And, make no mistake, the Ohio judicial system is in dire need of repair, as this book shows. At the time of writing this, I have served nearly nineteen years of my life on death row. If it hadn't been for supporters in the UK and around the world and my lawyers, I would probably have been strapped down years ago and had thousands of volts of electricity sent through my body.

To all who supported me and to my brother, Tom, who has been honest in communicating my story, I give my thanks. And, Tom, we don't always see eye to eye but I love you, brother.

Kenneth T. Richey

INTRODUCTION

This is the story of my brother, Kenny Richey. It is also an exposé of the American justice system and how one ambitious deputy prosecutor has, perhaps, perverted it to deprive a man of his freedom and, potentially, his life. It is a story of misery and a government's unwillingness to question its decisions. It is a story of survival. It is a story of the strength of one man's principles and how, if he'd betrayed them, he could have left the shadow of the executioner behind him many years ago. Above all, it is a true story.

In December 1982, eighteen-year-old Kenny Richey packed his troubles and the few possessions he had and left Scotland to seek his fortune in the so-called 'land of opportunity', the United States of America. In February 1985, weeks after my seventeenth birthday, I, like my brother before me, quit my low-wage Maggie Thatcher Youth Training Scheme job, hugged my mother goodbye and travelled to the State of Ohio to live temporarily with my American father.

In March 1986, while serving as a soldier in the US Army Airborne Rangers, I committed murder during a bad LSD trip. Condemned to serve a determinate sentence of sixty-five years in prison, I not only live with the burden of my actions, I also live with the burden that my actions contributed to the misfortune that befell my brother. As the prosecution suggested before a grand jury in my brother's case, 'If one brother is a murderer, it's likely the other is too.'

Ambitious Assistant Prosecutor Randall Basinger built the case against Kenny. When the grand jury convened in July 1986, for the purpose of determining whether charges should be brought against my brother, Assistant Prosecutor Randall Basinger was one of several candidates vying to be elected to wear the black robes of an Ohio State judge. The case Basinger mounted against Kenny earned him considerable publicity, as apparently it was designed to do. A capital murder trial in the predominantly farming and Bible-thumping community of Putnam County was scarcer than a UFO sighting. In fact, the last person charged of a capital offence in the county was a pig stealer in the mid nineteenth century. Found guilty by a jury of his peers, the man died hanging from the end of a rope.

The murder case against Kenny generated so much attention in Putnam County that, even years later, speculation persists between deckchairs of people sipping iced-tea under a hot sun – speculation as to whether a crime actually occurred in the early hours of June the thirtieth 1986 or whether the case against Kenny was the fabrication of a hungry assistant prosecutor seeking publicity.

If the latter is true, the publicity harvested from the murder indictment served its purpose. From schoolrooms to barrooms, people talked. In doing so, they broadcasted Basinger's name throughout the county. As a result, before Kenny's trial began on January the fifth 1987, Assistant Prosecutor Basinger was elected by the people of the county to the position and title of Judge Basinger.

Obviously, I, being Kenny's brother and a convicted murderer, have a vested interest in the telling of this story. You may question its integrity. It is for this reason that I initially refrained from writing the story in the hope that someone neutral might do it. I penned several letters to writers from my prison cell, providing them with the facts of my brother's case. Of the three who replied, one disbelieved that any person could be convicted on the evidence I presented and he suggested I hadn't been forthcoming with the truth. The other two considered the case too time consuming to investigate.

After years of frustration, I decided Kenny's story had to be told. I had to at least try to make amends for the predicament I unwittingly helped place my brother in. Yet, to be taken seriously, I knew I had to tell the story more objectively and factually than most writers would. I believe I have done that.

In pursuing the truth, I rarely relied on any one person's account of the facts where those facts are important and integral to events. In a sense, I'm bringing Kenny's case to trial again – a public trial whose jury consists of any reader opening this book. Is Kenny Richey innocent? That is for you to decide. To come to your decision, you need only the ability to read and the capacity to reason.

1

A STEP OUT OF LINE

Kenny pled guilty.

He pled guilty to one count of assault and one count of brandishing a weapon. His troubled ways trailed behind, beginning at the unruly age of fourteen with smashing a Pakistani corner-shop window for booze. Breaking open parking meters followed and then shoplifting, drunk and disorderly, assault . . . And four years after his sporadic trail of lawbreaking had begun, Kenny sat in another courtroom. This was not the Edinburgh courtroom he'd become only too familiar with but an American courtroom. At the time, he'd lived in the United States for just three months.

Despite his plea of guilty, he claims he was innocent. He claims he acted in self-defence. He and his American girlfriend got into an argument that led to the end of their short relationship. Kenny stormed from her house into the quiet residential streets of Ottawa, an isolated town in Ohio – population 20,000. Unknown to Kenny, the girl's father, accompanied by two friends he'd been drinking with, followed him.

They caught up with him. Mr Closson demanded his twenty-one-year-old daughter's ring that encircled a finger on Kenny's right hand. Kenny pulled the ring off and he threw it at Mr Closson's chest where it bounced to the pavement. This act of disrespect naturally enraged the man and, as soon as Mr Closson picked up the ring, Kenny alleges, the man charged him. A scuffle ensued and Mr Closson's friends joined in.

Overmatched, Kenny retreated and instinctively drew the flick knife he had found during a fishing trip. He never carried the knife for protection as the only danger you might encounter on Ottawa's streets was a mosquito bite. No, such knives are banned in the UK and he carried the push-button switchblade for the novelty of it.

As the court records show, he didn't use the knife after flicking the blade open – he just waved it in front of the three men. Kenny explained that he brandished it in an attempt to scare them so that he could make good his escape. The ploy failed. Apparently, the three men detected fear behind Kenny's bravado and they advanced on him. Kenny had never used a weapon on anyone – a record he failed to break on this occasion too. He tossed the knife to the gutter.

There is a dispute about who threw the first punch but one fact is known – Kenny delivered the worst of it. A woman, who witnessed the latter part of the fight from her porch, phoned the police. Within minutes, a deputy sheriff arrived in his patrol car. He arrested Kenny despite his plea of self-defence. Both of Mr Closson's friends needed medical attention. A gash on one man's brow required stitches and the other man was hospitalised with bruised and swollen testicles.

Kenny was booked into the Putnam County Jail on three counts of assault and one count of brandishing a weapon. His court-appointed attorney, Michael O'Malley, advised him that the offences carried a maximum prison sentence of fifteen years. In the following days, the opportunity for bail was offered to Kenny but he had little money as he had been living off our dad's wallet. Our dad, James Richey, an Ottawa resident, refused to bail Kenny out. He had hoped Kenny's move to America would end the cycle of him being in trouble with the law. He felt he'd done all he could to straighten Kenny out and nothing had worked so maybe a short stay in jail would achieve what he failed to.

In Edinburgh, where our dad had lived, on the few occasions when Kenny had brought the police to our door, Dad had disciplined him with the flat side of a wooden clothes brush over the backside. Yet, the punishment did nothing to curb the developing problem of Kenny getting into bother with the law. It was a problem our parents failed to recognise because they were consumed by other pressing problems – their disintegrating marriage and the demands of the family's failing coach charter business. Maybe it was because of these family problems that Kenny, feeling neglected, misbehaved in order to gain attention. As our family foundation crumbled, our younger brother, Steven, and I never acted up although we did turn on each other. But Kenny, it seemed, turned against the world.

By 1981, Dad had had enough. He packed a suitcase and left everything behind – his marriage of nineteen years, his family, his broken business and Scotland, the country he called home. He returned to America where he'd been raised and where some of his family lived, scattered throughout the State of Ohio.

When Kenny stepped on to American soil on December the twenty-fourth 1982, Dad hoped he had left his rebelliousness behind and, for several weeks following his arrival, it appeared he had. They spent most of their time together, fishing, camping, driving around, sightseeing and visiting friends and relatives. But Kenny soon became restless in the small town environment.

As a town, Ottawa offered little entertainment. It had no nightclubs, no takeaways and no places to dance to the latest music and meet people his own age. The jukeboxes in the few bars and taverns played country and western. The town was as stagnant as a picture postcard in time.

However, during the 1980s, America was being intravenously injected with drug imports and even this Bible-Belt community was being infiltrated by pushers, as were all communities which had idle young people with money to spend. Soon, Kenny began staggering to our dad's doorstep, his belly bloated with beer and his head buzzing from illegal substances. Although this behaviour did decrease when he began seeing Laura Closson, it didn't stop. It disturbed Dad who rarely drank and never used drugs. He tried talking some sense into Kenny but Kenny responded by saying that he was overreacting. That was in the days before Kenny phoned from the Putnam County Sheriff's Office.

Days after his arrest, he pled guilty to one count of assault and one count of brandishing a weapon. He accepted what is known as a 'plea bargain', which is an integral tool of the American criminal system. The plea bargain gives an accused the opportunity to plead guilty in exchange for reduced charges or a reduced sentence that he might not otherwise receive if he takes his case to trial and loses. If properly used, the accused and the prosecution can, theoretically, reach mutually agreeable terms. The State benefits by eliminating the expense incurred by a trial and any potential appeal costs while the accused benefits from a reduced sentence.

But the plea-bargain process, like anything else, is sometimes abused. Prosecutors threaten the accused with the maximum sentence he might theoretically but not actually receive if he is found guilty following a trial. The accused, often ignorant and scared, is persuaded by the threat and accepts the plea bargain, even when he may, in fact, be innocent of the charges.

The fifteen-year sentence that Attorney O'Malley advised Kenny he could receive if found guilty on all charges was an unrealistic claim. In reality, if found guilty on all counts, at the age of eighteen and on a first offence (as far as the American courts were concerned), Kenny faced, at most, a few weeks in jail and a couple of years on probation. Ignorant, Kenny pled guilty in exchange for two months in jail – hardly a bargain at all.

After he received the two-month sentence, Kenny claims that Assistant Prosecutor Randall Basinger approached the defence table. He asserts that Basinger nodded at O'Malley then faced Kenny and said, 'If you ever step out of line in my county again, I'll get you.'

'What was that all about?' Kenny claims to have asked O'Malley after Basinger withdrew. O'Malley supposedly told him that Basinger was friendly with Mr Closson. Being a friend of Mr Closson is something Basinger later did not refute. But whether Basinger did actually threaten Kenny is difficult to prove. Even if he had made the threat, it's doubtful he remembered years later. Or did he? Whatever the case, three years after meeting Basinger, Kenny would, once again, look at the man across a courtroom – not to accept another plea bargain but to battle for his life. Following his two-month plea-bargained sentence, Kenny had decided one thing – he would never again plead guilty to a crime when he was innocent.

It is a principle that he would risk his life itself to uphold.

2

LAND OF OPPORTUNITY

Upon Kenny's release from jail in May 1983, our dad, then working for a photography company, hired him to work as his assistant. Dad's job involved travelling around the United States and he disliked the idea of leaving Kenny alone in Ottawa. He believed the assault conviction would lead to further trouble with the law. In Edinburgh, as in most cities, repeat offenders go relatively unnoticed. In Ottawa, the police would keep an eye on Kenny, maybe even harass him occasionally – lawmen in rural towns don't take too kindly to outsiders bringing city traits into their domain. If Kenny so much as curled his lip at a passing police cruiser, Dad feared Kenny would find himself in handcuffs again.

He also hired Kenny because the travel involved would offer him the opportunity to experience more than he could in Ottawa, where a few rounds of crazy golf on a Friday evening was an exciting night out for many in the township. Dad also believed that a job would instil some responsibility in Kenny as well as put some money in his pocket.

The work entailed travelling to a designated city where Dad would lease some temporary office space. Then he'd hire a small staff whose job was to call all the names on a lengthy list to arrange for the people to come in to have their family pictures taken. A photographer would then arrive in the city a week or two later to begin snapping photographs.

Kenny and our dad travelled together for a couple of months and Kenny worked hard. It seemed that the job was the perfect pick-me-up he needed to gain confidence in the adult world. After two months, he received an offer to be a photographer's assistant. He was interested in photography and he believed the assistant's position could be a stepping stone to better things. An added bonus was an increase in pay. Although it meant splitting up from our dad, he accepted the job, believing in the promise of a career in photography.

He travelled with the photographer, Bob Grogan, until December and stopped for two weeks at Christmas. He spent the fortnight with our dad and, in early January, they hugged and separated. Dad travelled west and Kenny rejoined Bob and the pair headed north.

However, any aspirations Kenny had to begin a career in photography were fleeting. Within one week of entering Brainerd, Minnesota, he had fallen in love. Two weeks later, Bob left Brainerd alone as Kenny had got engaged to be married. He enlisted in the United States Marine Corps which he was able to do because of the US naturalisation he had received almost automatically at birth because our dad was a US citizen.

Kenny recalls those two weeks as a whirlwind of emotions. 'I could see my life with this woman ahead of me,' he said, 'and I was happy with the image.' Aged twenty-eight and eight years his senior, Wendy Amerud had met Kenny at a party. A lifelong Brainerd resident, Wendy could be described as a reserved woman of slight build with a sprinkle of light freckles over her cheeks. As a couple, Wendy and Kenny were the epitome of the term 'opposites attract'. Wendy was a homebody – she wanted to settle down and raise a family. Kenny was outgoing and acted like the end of the world seemed imminent. He liked partying and dancing. So news of the engagement surprised our family. We didn't believe the marriage would last more than a year but we supported him in the way that families do and it was more a case of being obliged to than anything else. In the face of this, Kenny married Wendy on May the twenty-sixth 1984, after toughing out months of Marine Corps training in San Diego, California.

He claims his decision to enlist in the marines was a practical one – the travelling assistant photographer's job was unsuitable for a married man. However, he lacked qualifications for a decent job and the marines were willing to train him in a skill he could apply in civilian life. There was also the additional benefit that they would provide housing and medical assistance for Wendy.

One week before the wedding, Mum, our younger brother, Steven, and I met Dad at a Minnesota airport. It was the first time we had seen him since he'd left Scotland in 1981. The four of us drove together to Brainerd for the wedding and checked into a Holiday Inn. My parents discarded their differences during the reunion and our time together remained peaceful.

As weddings go, Kenny and Wendy's was a tense affair. I believe all who attended would agree with that. Residual tension carried over from the night before when Wendy's Vietnam veteran brother had slapped Kenny. As so often is the case, alcohol had been the root cause of the altercation. All the guests had gathered in a bar to celebrate the forthcoming wedding. Throughout the night, Wendy's brother repeatedly asked Kenny if he was going to take good care of his sister. Tiring of the offensive question, Kenny said, 'Man, why don't ye shut up with that?' And that's when he slapped Kenny.

Kenny kept his wits about him. He didn't retaliate, fearing that, if he had, half the guests might have shown up at the wedding with broken noses and black eyes. So he stood there, numbed by booze, saying, 'Go ahead – take another shot if it will make you feel better.' It may have set the tone for the marriage.

A few days after they exchanged vows, the newly married couple drove south to Camp Lejune, North Carolina, for Kenny's six-month duty assignment. But, within a month of their arrival, the flaws that were to cause the deterioration of their marriage had already appeared.

Wendy missed home a lot. It was only natural considering that she'd lived with her parents in Brainerd for all of her twenty-eight years. Also, she'd been unprepared for having to share Kenny with the Marines Corps quite as much as she had to. His duties consumed ten to fourteen hours of his time every weekday, leaving little time for Wendy. His long absences accentuated her loneliness and Kenny discovered the extent of Wendy's homesickness when he received their first telephone bill for calls made from their off-camp flat. It topped $1000 – nearly twice as much as he earned in a month. It triggered their first row. Days later, Wendy left for Brainerd. They had been together just six weeks.

Then, ten weeks after she left, she returned. Determined to make the marriage work, she was also desperate to prove her family's reservations about the marriage wrong. In an attempt to help matters, prior to completing his training as a heavy vehicle driver, Kenny requested a duty assignment in Minnesota. If his request was approved, Wendy's home town would then be just a short drive away. However, upon completing his training, Kenny received orders to report for duty at Camp Pendleton, California – about as far from Minnesota as you can go without leaving the continental United States.

Allotted twenty days' leave, they travelled north. They stayed in Ottawa for two days and then spent twelve days in Brainerd, before driving to California. Upon reaching the State, they rented a semi-furnished mobile home near Camp Pendleton and, on that same day, Private First Class Richey reported for duty. Given relief of duty for the day, he returned to the mobile home to unpack.

Soon after, a man dressed in fatigues with stripes stopped by. He introduced himself as Kenny's gunnery sergeant. Kenny had arrived at the right time, the sergeant told him. A vacancy in the sergeant's ten-pin bowling team needed to be filled. The team was playing that night and the sergeant invited Kenny to the camp bowling alley to play a rival team. 'And bring your wife, too,' the sergeant added.

Politely, Kenny declined. He'd never bowled before and, besides, he still had unpacking to do.

His gunnery sergeant straightened as if insulted. 'It isn't an invitation, Marine. It's an order. I'll see you there, seven sharp.'

The evening didn't go well. Any chance Kenny had of re-instating fair relations with his sergeant diminished with each gutterball he made – and he made many. It might have helped if Kenny had acted like he gave his best but, embarrassed, he laughed and made jokes about his performance. Unfortunately, his gunnery sergeant was a serious bowler. Wendy didn't help either. Annoyed at having to attend the bowling match, she behaved in an aloof manner, altogether ignoring the other marine wives.

Due to Kenny's deficient performance, the second squad of the third platoon of the Marine Transport Battalion lost their bowling match, dropped one position in the league standings and lost the squad's collected wager of $300. One week later, Kenny received an Article-15 disciplinary report. He was reported for being late for zero-six-thirty formation every day of the week. His gunnery sergeant cited the infraction. Kenny claims he made formation every morning with minutes to spare but he held his tongue at the hearing. The hearing officer reprimanded him and fined him $50. The payback, Kenny believed, would satisfy the sergeant. But, one week later, he again stood before the hearing officer accused of formation lateness. He wanted to complain and explain the situation with his sergeant but he knew, if he questioned the integrity of a

13

non-commissioned officer, he'd face serious consequences. He kept his mouth shut and received a fine of $100.

He had trouble on the home front too. Wendy constantly suggested he quit the marines so they could return to Brainerd. Depressed, she began visiting the camp psychologist. It confused Kenny. 'If she was having problems, she should have talked to me rather than some stranger,' he said of her visits.

The problem, she countered, was him and the marines. Only if they moved to Brainerd, she said, would they be able to save their marriage.

They spent less time together and then, to complicate matters, Wendy confirmed that she was pregnant. She had been carrying the baby for two-and-a-half months. Yet, any chance of their relationship being revived by the pregnancy died when Wendy demanded that the baby be born in Brainerd.

Following another of many arguments over the baby's birthplace, Kenny stomped from their home and drove to Camp Pendleton. There, he visited the bowling alley which was the local marine hangout. He was dismayed to see his gunnery sergeant's all-terrain truck sitting in the parking lot but he went in to the bowling alley anyway. He spent an hour in the video games room then drifted to the bar and drank a pitcher of beer.

As always, the facility bristled with people. He wandered amongst them, debating whether to return to face Wendy again or spend more quarters on the video games, when he noticed his gunnery sergeant drinking and bowling with lads from his platoon. The sergeant sneered at him, then turned to the others and said something that made them laugh in Kenny's direction. Angered, Kenny headed for the exit. Just inside the door, bowling balls were racked along the walls. He took one. It was the same bowling ball his gunnery sergeant found on the driver's seat of his Bronco, surrounded by fragments of what had been the side window.

He stopped by a chemist on the way home and bought

vitamins for Wendy – they had agreed she should take them during pregnancy. Next to the vitamins stood a column of a familiar brand of travel sickness pills. What cheaper way to forget things for a while? He bought a packet of the pills. They were the same pills he and his mates had often taken back in Edinburgh, sometimes before a party, sometimes on a camping trip. Ingested in quantity, the pills produce a weird hallucinogenic high and several hours of oblivion. Before he drove home, he swallowed ten of the pills in the car and washed them down with a can of beer – a mix the pill packet warned against.

He arrived home and entered the kitchen where Wendy sat, writing another tome to her family. He sat across the kitchen table from her, smoking a cigarette. Her expression told him she still held a grudge from their earlier argument and he could only imagine what she was writing to her family about. The last thing he remembered was getting up after Wendy had asked him if he intended to see about a discharge from the marines. He collapsed and lay unconscious on the floor. He awoke moments before doctors pumped his stomach at a civilian hospital. A short time later, he was released on his own recognisance.

On the drive home from the hospital, Wendy started on him. He said nothing. He just sat there, taking the verbal blows, knowing he probably deserved them. 'It's time you grew up,' she said. 'I'm pregnant. Fun time is over. All you want to do is play soldier, get soused and cause problems that's no good for me or the baby.' She started crying and Kenny felt helpless.

'I couldn't just quit the marines like it was some nine-to-five job. She was demanding the impossible,' he said of that time.

She told him she was sick of everything. 'You'd better see about a discharge. I mean it. If you don't, then I'm going home.'

They rode the rest of the journey in silence.

The following morning, a Thursday, Kenny was assigned the menial task of minding the barracks' front desk. When he returned home that evening, he found Wendy solemn and quiet. It lasted the whole evening but he considered it a relief from the constant needling.

At zero-nine-hundred hours the following morning, the company first sergeant called Kenny to his office. Upon entering, Kenny snapped to attention. An officer, a major, occupied a chair to the left of the sergeant's desk. Behind the major stood two military policemen.

'At ease,' the sergeant said.

He relaxed, clasping his hands behind his back. The sergeant told him he was confined to the battalion area for the weekend.

'For what reason, First Sergeant?'

The sergeant turned to the major but the officer shook his head. He faced Kenny and shrugged. 'Let's just say it has something to do with the past and something to do with the future.'

Confused, Kenny told him he couldn't abide by the confinement order, saying that he had a pregnant wife at home who may need him.

'Then you leave us no choice but to place you in the brig for the weekend.'

His pleas fell on deaf ears.

He did not learn of the reason for his confinement until Sunday afternoon, when an MP escorted him from his cell to a bare room with a wall phone. The MP gave him a slip of paper that had a telephone number scribbled on it and instructed him to call.

Wendy answered.

'Where the bloody hell are you?' Kenny asked.

'In a motel,' she replied, her voice strained. 'I'm going home today. I've packed our stuff and I'm taking it with me in a U-haul.'

She told him she had dropped his clothing off at the barracks and, before hanging up, she added that he should call her in a week or two at her mother's. She still loved him, she said – maybe they could work things out.

The following morning, he sat before the major he met in the sergeant's office. If the telephone call had failed to stun him, the words of the officer did not. He listened, barely able to speak, as the major told him he was being discharged.

'A discharge? For what?'

'A mental disorder.'

The major, Wendy's psychologist, went on to explain that Wendy had reported that he had taken an overdose of pills as a suicide attempt after she threatened to leave him – hence the stomach pump at the civilian hospital.

After the major conferred with Kenny's supervisors, his discharge was decided. His performance had been rated poor because of the two Article-15s and his gunnery sergeant's evaluation reports showed him to be below average. He tried to explain the incident that had led to his stomach being pumped and his personal problems with his gunnery sergeant but he received no sympathy. The Marine Corps had made its decision.

Kenny remembers the period as one of the worst in his life. He'd tried hard to put his troubled ways behind him, to stand on his own feet and shoulder adult responsibilities – only to have his legs cut from under him. Never had he hated anyone as much as he hated Wendy then.

His honourable discharge took three weeks to be processed and, during that time, he was confined to camp. It was an order he didn't question as the alternative would have been three weeks in the brig. He did little more than lie around, licking his wounds. Both his military career and his marriage, it seemed, were over. Wendy had seen to that and he didn't know if he could forgive her. Yet, he knew he wasn't entirely blameless. He could have tried harder; he should have been more responsible, more attentive to her needs. Their marriage was now in ashes. The one positive thing that was rising from the ashes was their child. And, for the sake of their child, he decided that he would follow Wendy to Brainerd, try to make things work, try to do the right thing.

He phoned her several times during the three weeks he was confined to camp and they reconciled. He swallowed the animosity he felt towards her and tried to digest it. When his discharge became final in the spring, he travelled to Brainerd with little more than the clothes on his back. He wished he could say that the Amerud family welcomed him with open arms and were willing to support him but they merely tolerated him. He moved in with Wendy at her mother's house. It became an uncomfortable situation because Wendy's mother blamed him for the troubled state of her daughter's marriage and he was unable to find steady work which only made matters worse. Wendy and her mother's criticisms grew frequent and her mother's tolerance waned. It affected his self-esteem.

On October the twenty-eighth 1985, Wendy delivered a healthy boy. They named the child Sean and, though the birth boosted his spirits, the effect was short-lived. As the months passed and he was still unemployed, he began to feel resented by Wendy and her mother. The small house became claustrophobic. He started arguing with Wendy over the smallest things. He began to find more excuses to stay away. He felt like an intruder in their home. Depression set in as he reflected on his station in life. He was nearing the age of twenty-one and in a broken marriage. He had no job and nothing to show for those twenty-one years except for a child he couldn't support as much as he wanted to. He'd travelled from the UK for this? He began to drink more, take drugs, undo the scaffold that kept him upright.

In January 1986, he had a final fight with Wendy. It was the war to end all wars and parting words by those who were tired of maintaining the pretence of a marriage were fired by both sides. As their anger echoed in each other's ears, they knew their marriage was over. Kenny called Dad and asked him to meet him at the Lima Greyhound Bus Station. The next day, he hopped on to a Greyhound.

With each passing mile, he sank further into the seat, further into himself. Reality hit. He'd somehow managed to screw up everything and here he was again, with little money, dependent on our dad. When he got off the bus in the small city of Lima, Ohio, he no longer felt like himself. Failure suffocated him and he just wanted to forget. Even Dad noticed the difference in Kenny when he met him at the bus station and drove him the thirteen miles to Columbus Grove and the Old Farm Village Apartment Complex where our dad was living at the time. He couldn't put his finger on it but there was definitely a difference in him.

Less than one month later, Kenny attempted suicide.

3

DAZED AND CONFUSED

Kenny did little following his return from Minnesota – except talk. He talked of returning for his son and he talked of returning to Edinburgh but he did nothing towards achieving these goals. He was twenty-one years old and he felt like an old boxer with no fight left in him. Instead of trying to find work, to climb back on to his feet, he moped around our dad's apartment. Dad quickly tired of this and urged Kenny to find work even though the small town of four thousand people offered too few jobs. Still, he wanted to see Kenny at least make an effort. But Kenny signed on for government welfare and, to get out from under Dad's feet, he began socialising and drinking with the other aimless young people around town.

Our dad didn't approve. Kenny slept late into the mornings after staggering into the apartment in the dead of night, usually waking Dad up in the process. Kenny wasn't the first person to be tripped up by life and Dad talked to him one morning, telling him to straighten up but his words went unheeded. So Dad decided to act. The next time Kenny staggered back to the flat, he found the door locked. He banged on the door but Dad ignored him, as difficult as it was, and Kenny ended up sleeping the night on the doorstep. Despite this measure, Kenny didn't change his ways. A few days later, Dad packed Kenny's clothes and dropped them off in a motel room he rented for Kenny for one night in Ottowa, four miles from Columbus Grove. He hoped the sudden lack of support would jolt Kenny to his feet.

The day after our dad kicked Kenny out of the apartment, Kenny walked to the government welfare office and informed them of his situation. The welfare office rented him a room for three days in the Skylark Motel. A cheap motel, it was infamous for cockroach infestation. In reality, a guest probably saw a single roach scurrying for darkness when they switched on a light, during a nightly visit to the bathroom, and, soon afterwards, the town knew it as Cockroach Motel – such is the nature of small-town gossip that Kenny would become so familiar with.

After three days in the motel, he would be on his own. All the government provided after the three days' emergency housing was sympathy. On the third day, he cut himself with a razorblade. Depression had carried him to a nearby park where he bled on the grass. He'd nicked an arterial vein. Fortunately, the first person to notice him, an off-duty deputy, drove him to St Rita's Medical Center in Lima. The police contacted our dad who rushed to the hospital. He blamed himself for Kenny's actions yet he believed Kenny needed the kind of help that he was obviously unable to provide. A day later, after much consideration, he filed commitment papers with the court and, two days after that, Kenny was shackled and chained like a prisoner and taken from the hospital to the State mental institution in Toledo. There, he underwent a series of psychiatric tests.

Almost immediately, our dad regretted his decision. Maybe he should have been more understanding and more patient? After all, when his nineteen years of marriage failed, he spent some time coming to terms with the failure. Yet, he never tried to kill himself. This he couldn't understand. What sane person tries to kill himself? In our dad's mind, Kenny suffered from mental problems. Maybe the doctors at the State institution could help?

However, after a couple of weeks, finding that Kenny wasn't a danger to himself or to others, the institution released him. They recommended that he seek therapy on a regular basis. It was a recommendation he thumbed his nose at. Dad picked Kenny up from the institution. The drive was long and silent – Kenny felt betrayed by him.

He got his old room back and, as the days passed, it appeared that his attitude had, indeed, changed for the better. He still went out but mainly on the weekends and, when he staggered into the apartment, he quietly headed to his room. He even found work in a factory but he was laid off after a few weeks for being a non-union member. Although back on benefit, he managed to save the airfare home. As May passed into June, he decided he would fly home in July.

It was around this time that he met Peggy Price and Hope Collins. Twenty-eight-year-old Peggy and twenty-one-year-old Hope, both unemployed single mothers, were residents and neighbours of A-building in the apartment complex where our dad stayed. The complex consisted of three white buildings, each two storeys high. The doors of Hope and Peggy's first-floor apartments faced each other, separated only by the wood planking of the open breezeway landing. Kenny met Peggy first through the elder of Peggy's two daughters, nine-year-old Angela. Kenny was popular with the kids at the apartment complex. Occasionally, he could be found playing football with them. Few adults seemed to have any time for the kids and Kenny could relate to how the kids felt. He sensed that our parents, who had both worked, didn't have enough time for him when he was growing up.

Peggy and Kenny struck up a friendship right away and, within days of meeting, Kenny began spending most of each day at Peggy's apartment. They talked, drank coffee and listened to music or watched the movie channel. In the evening, other friends of Peggy usually visited, sometimes bringing a few beers. Kenny and Peggy were only friends. Peggy had a number of friends – though the term 'friend' must be used loosely because none of the friendships appeared particularly strong. Peggy and Hope's flats were the usual gathering places and it was only fitting for those drifting to the scene to befriend their hosts.

At sixteen stone, Peggy could be mistaken for a short portly man if her dark lifeless shoulder-length hair had been cropped. Her face, pale and doughy, had the beginnings of a moustache. Still, appearances aside, she was popular, probably due to her bubbly personality and her open-door policy. Like Peggy, her neighbour, skinny, blonde stringy-haired Hope Collins, regularly opened her door for all-comers. Often, both of their doors remained open at the same time, allowing people to drift from one apartment to the other. Hope's apartment welcomed drug use whereas Peggy's did not. Hope herself was a drug user and that was the main reason her husband, Robert Collins, had left her one year before.

Robert Collins had taken their two-year-old daughter with him but Hope called the police who returned little Cynthia two days later. To this day, Robert regrets not fighting to retain custody of his child.

Kenny first saw Hope when he was sitting with Peggy, looking over the rail of the breezeway landing. Hope passed below, tramping along the pavement. Peggy commented, 'Look at that trollop. She walks everywhere in her bare feet. And I bet you she's left that poor kid alone in her apartment again.'

Hope often seemed to neglect her child, leaving Cynthia alone for hours. She did this despite returning from the apartment complex laundry room one day to discover that Cynthia had set her bed on fire with a lighter. And this was not an isolated incident – Cynthia had a history of burning things. It may be the reason why Hope began the habit of feeding her two-year-old tranquilisers. That way, she would sleep when she was left alone. Going a step further, Hope fitted a locking device on the outside of Cynthia's bedroom door to keep her inside. Hope's practices did not go undetected. On two occasions, Becky Leader from the Putnam County Children's Services visited her. The first visit concerned Hope's neglect of her child. The second visit was regarding Hope administering drugs to Cynthia. Hope denied the accusations and, without proof, Becky Leader could do nothing more.

Defiantly, Hope persisted in her ways, becoming vociferously angry at the government for sticking their nose in her business. She seemed unconcerned by the dangers of her behaviour and was much more interested in discovering the identity of the person or persons who repeatedly reported her to the authorities. Any suspicions she had, she kept to herself. Obviously, more than one person witnessed her behaviour otherwise she would have known the identity of the person who reported her. As it turned out, Hope did indeed know who reported her. She learned, some months later, that it was her friend, Peggy Price.

Peggy introduced Hope to Kenny during the first week of June at the Columbus Grove June Jubilee Fair. Then, they said little more than 'Hi, it's nice to meet you.' But, over the following weeks, they became better acquainted. As with his relationship with Peggy, Hope and Kenny's relationship remained platonic and, until around June the fifteenth, Kenny, Hope and Peggy frequently spent time together.

Their days were predictable. In the morning, the three convened at Peggy or Hope's apartment and they started the day with coffee, accompanied by the latest gossip. Gossip is ubiquitous in most American small towns and almost has the status of a pastime in some apartment complexes. Like a daily soap opera, all the latest scandals entered small talk and laundry-room conversation. For Kenny, Peggy and Hope, subjects included who had screwed who – in more ways than one –

whose relationship was on the rocks and, during the month of June, my violent actions of over two months before were fully aired. Unfortunately, Kenny trusted the wrong people.

Known simply as 'Kenny's brother', the apartment rumour mill ensured that I progressed from the one who shot two people during a bad LSD trip to a drug-crazed 'Rambo' character on a killing spree. As the titbits passed from mouth to ear, each one added a new twist to the story – such is the nature of gossip.

As the days aged at the complex and visitors accumulated at Peggy or Hope's apartments, a party often ensued. Sometimes Kenny participated, sometimes he refrained. Life in Columbus Grove was very different from his clubbing and pub-crawling days with the lads back in Edinburgh. 'A time of recuperation' is how he described it. He saved what money he could and counted down his days until his departure in July. He planned to find work in Edinburgh driving lorries, which was what he'd learned to do in the marines. He'd given up the hope of taking his son with him but maybe, in time and through child support payments, some civility could be established between him and Wendy to allow him a relationship with his son.

Meantime, Kenny had very little money coming in and in order to keep at least a little independence he went camping a lot. Ohio's summer nights were warm and all he needed was a sleeping bag. Usually he camped for a couple of days at a time, three hundred yards from the apartment complex in woods that were split in two by a freshwater burn. The trees were completely surrounded by a sea of head-high cornstalks. Sometimes, he went alone but, more often, he took a handful of kids from the complex. Those kids whined during the week and a half, from June the fifteenth to the twenty-fifth, because Kenny wouldn't take them camping. During that time, other things were occupying Kenny's mind – specifically, the body of nineteen-year-old Candy Barchet, the woman he would be accused of attempting to murder on June the thirtieth.

4

EYE CANDY

Divorcée Candy Barchet moved into the empty apartment below Hope Collins's place with her one-year-old son, Jason, on June the fifteenth. Peggy and Kenny sipped coffee as they talked in Peggy's living room when news of the arriving tenants was carried by the giddy voice of Peggy's daughter, Angela. 'Mommy, mommy, a lady moved into the apartment downstairs and she's got a really cute boy. Come see – hurry.'

Peggy, followed by Kenny, descended the stairs and welcomed the new neighbour. Kenny found petite Candy attractive. Obviously, it was a mutual feeling because a sexual relationship ensued between them the next day. The affair began with an explosion of lust but, when the hormones settled about a week later, the element of attraction faded. As Kenny recalls, 'She was fun but it was no more than that. Candy knew I was going home in a few weeks so we had no notions of developing a serious relationship.'

For Candy too, the relationship may have been purely self-serving. She benefited because her intimacy with Kenny gained her a social leg-up in her new environment. Maybe she needed that because, within a week of her arrival, her reputation followed her in the form of words like 'slut' and 'floozie'.

A few days after Candy moved in to the complex, she shuffled into Peggy's flat where she and Kenny were again sitting chatting. Distraught, crying and rubbing a blemish on her cheek, she told them that her ex-boyfriend had appeared and started an argument that ended with him slapping her around her new apartment. Enraged, Kenny stormed out of Peggy's door and looked for the man. Unable to find him, he returned ten minutes later. He consoled the still upset Candy, assuring her that, if the man hurt her again, he'd kill him. Kenny described the incident as no more than talk – male chest-pounding. Still, it was a statement that would return to bruise his character.

A second commotion involving Candy occurred on June the twenty-fourth. Kenny had decided to go camping that afternoon because the kids had been grumbling at him and he had begun to lose interest in Candy. As he told it, he was put off by her frequent fibbing.

He walked to Hope's flat that morning for their routine chat and coffee and soon they were joined by Peggy and Candy. He wore his baggy camouflage trousers and lightweight boots but not necessarily because of his intended camping trip – he was keeping his other clothes clean for going home. Also, camouflage gear was in style that year in America where fashion-conscious New Yorkers paid as much as a hundred dollars for bona fide military fatigue trousers.

Shortly before noon, Peggy, Hope and Kenny followed Candy downstairs to her apartment where they planned to listen to Candy's record collection. Within half an hour, John Butler and Mike Heit, two of Hope's friends, appeared at Candy's doorstep. Peggy's daughters, who were playing outside, had told the men where they could find Hope. John Butler beamed from behind the screen door, revealing a half-gallon jar of whisky. 'Party time!' he said and laughed.

Minutes later, Peggy, Candy, John and Mike huddled around the coffee table, drinking double shots of whisky, chased down by a cola. Hope and Kenny refrained.

After eight shots, Candy stopped drinking and lay back on

her chair, burping. 'I feel dizzy,' she said. She rested her bare feet on the table.

'Oh-oh, tootsies,' John said. He began massaging Candy's feet. 'You don't mind, do ya, bud?' he said to Kenny.

'Why should I mind?' Kenny replied. He felt some distaste at the early drinking. He was particularly disappointed with Peggy, whose kids were playing just outside the door. He rose and said, 'Well, I'm off camping.'

As he walked from the apartment, Peggy, John and Mike continued with their drinking session. Outside, on the grass, Kenny wrestled with some of the neighbourhood kids for five minutes or so. He then strolled past B-building that stood between A-building and C-building – the three blocks formed a letter I shape. He then sauntered into our dad's ground-floor apartment in C-building.

Apparently nauseous, Candy pulled herself from her chair, staggered into the hall, passing the bedroom where her son slept, and into the bathroom with seconds to spare before vomiting. She swayed out the door and went into her bedroom where she collapsed on the bed.

Peggy also visited the bathroom. On her return, she paused by Candy's door to see if she was OK. Candy asked her to fetch a rag and a pan. After she returned with the requested items, she closed Candy's door and retreated to the living room. Minutes after Peggy sat down, John stood up. He was a big man and he wore an unseasonably heavy leather motorcycle jacket. He shrugged it from his frame and then he too visited the bathroom.

Presumably after what must have seemed like an age with John failing to return, Hope remarked that one of them should check to see if he was all right. No one volunteered so she got up and went into the hall. She found the bathroom door ajar but the bathroom empty. She moved the few paces to Candy's closed door and she listened. Hearing nothing, she cracked open the door and then quickly shut it again. Inside, she had seen John's head between Candy's naked thighs.

She told Peggy and Mike what she had just seen and they chuckled. Mike turned up the volume of the stereo and heavy metal music squealed from the speakers. Moments later, Peggy's daughter waltzed into the apartment with her sister in tow. They asked for money for the ice-cream man.

'You don't need ice cream. You'll ruin your appetites,' Peggy said.

The kids pleaded but Peggy remained firm.

'Where's Ken?' Angela asked.

'I think he went home. Don't go bothering him for money.'

Angela said she wouldn't. She asked where 'Biker John' was. Peggy told her he was with Candy in her room. Angela's eyes widened and she darted out of the room. Peggy faced Hope and raised a brow. Hope shrugged and lit a cigarette.

Upon entering our dad's, Kenny told him he was going camping and said, if the neighbour's kids came to the door, he should tell them he'd come back for them after dinner. He smoked a cigarette and then packed a few bits of clothing, throwing some cans of beans into his rucksack. He didn't bother with a tent – he slept in a spacious lean-to he and the kids had built from fallen tree limbs. Finally, he strapped an army survival knife to his belt.

He stepped out of the apartment with the rucksack hanging loosely from his shoulder. He turned left through the ground-floor breezeway and headed for the wall of cornstalks that ran along the edge of the apartment complex property some thirty yards ahead. Before he could disappear among the stalks, the slap of small feet resounded against the concrete behind him. He turned.

'Ken, Ken,' Angela said, obviously distraught.

Kenny claims that the girl cried a tirade of words so fast he couldn't understand her. All he could make out were the words

'Candy' and 'bedroom'. He reacted. He sprinted back through the breezeway, dropped the rucksack on our dad's doorstep and shot over the grassy field, heading for Candy's ground-floor apartment.

He threw open the screen door and double-stepped through the living room into the hall, barely glancing at Peggy, Hope or Mike Heit. As Kenny approached, John Butler stepped from Candy's bedroom grinning. He pushed past the man and looked into the room. Candy lay across the bed, looking no worse for wear. Angela had been so upset that Kenny thought maybe Candy's ex-boyfriend had paid her another visit or that something equally serious had happened.

John Butler glowered at him. He said, 'If ya wanna fight, go ahead.' Butler noticed the survival knife hanging from Kenny's belt. 'I hope ya didn't plan on using that on me, punk, 'cause I'll stick it up your British ass.'

Kenny stuttered – he was confused as he'd expected an entirely different scene to meet his eyes. Yet, Butler had challenged him – but the moron was drunk. He wavered in front of Kenny, his bulk blocking any exit. Kenny only weighed about twelve stone and Butler was at least four stone heavier than him. He knew he wouldn't be able to bowl the man over. He drew the knife from its scabbard and threw it on to the floor behind him, saying, 'I don't want to hurt ye.'

Butler lunged. Kenny ducked and came up, punching Butler on the side of his head. The blow had had little effect and Butler got his hands on Kenny, using his weight to slam him against the wall. Kenny kneed him in the groin, once, twice, and Butler slithered to the floor, taking Kenny down with him. They rolled over the floor into the living room, knocking over furniture and grunting. Peggy got out of her chair and rushed from the apartment. Mike Heit watched. Hope tried separating them, only to be pushed on to her backside. After a couple of minutes of wrestling, each gasped for air. Kenny gripped Butler in a headlock and, finally, Butler gasped, 'I'll quit if you quit?'

Kenny nodded and tentatively let go of the man. They lay almost side by side, chests heaving. When Kenny dragged himself to his feet, he said, 'That was stupid.' He retrieved his knife and, before leaving the apartment, he punched the wall, angry that he could have been goaded into behaving like that. He immediately suspected that the blow to his hand had broken a bone in his pinkie.

That evening, not wanting to disappoint his neighbour's three boys, he went camping despite his swollen, throbbing hand. However, as soon as morning crept into the woods, he returned to the apartment complex with the groggy kids in tow. His hand ached. Our dad drove him to the medical centre in Lima – the closest hospital to Columbus Grove. X-rays confirmed the broken bone. His pinkie and ring finger were wrapped to a solid temporary brace that extended from just below his elbow to his fingers and painkillers were prescribed.

That evening of June the twenty-fifth, after Hope, Peggy and a few others left Candy's apartment, Kenny stayed at Candy's request. If she wanted to discuss the previous day's incident involving Butler, he had little to say. Nothing needed saying. As far as he was concerned, he'd had fun but now it was over between them.

She told him she wished to continue their friendship. He had no problem with that. 'Strictly platonic,' he agreed.

At no time, Candy later confessed during Kenny's murder trial, did Kenny object to their platonic relationship – he never expressed anger or showed hostility towards her because of it. In fact, Candy agreed that Kenny just went his way and she hers. But this didn't mean they avoided each other – after all, they both socialised with Peggy and Hope. Kenny still talked to Candy and they both remained civil.

Inevitably, Candy found a new toy to play with. Twenty-eight-year-old Mike Nichols was a bit slow, having only been educated up to primary two level. Arriving at the apartment complex on June the twenty-eighth from the distant town of Ironton, he had come to stay with his mum who lived there. He'd visited his mum at the complex before and knew Peggy and Hope. This time, he planned to stay for a couple of weeks and attend his brother's wedding. On the day he got there, Peggy introduced him to Candy and they hit it off.

Sunday June the twenty-ninth would be a long day. For some, the day ended at around one o'clock in the morning of the thirtieth but, for others, the day has never ended – for that day brought tragedy, death and years of misery.

Kenny arrived at Hope's flat at approximately six o'clock in the evening. It was a hot, muggy night and Hope, Peggy and Kenny escaped the stuffy apartment to the breezeway landing with a six-pack. It was only half an hour later when Peggy's boyfriend, thirty-two-year-old Bob Dannenberg, appeared. He had a twelve-pack of beer with him and he passed the cold cans around. After Candy and Mike Nichols came up on to the breezeway, the supply of beer soon dwindled so Hope suggested, 'Let's get more beer and have a party!'

Her suggestion received no opposition. The evening began in the same way as many evenings preceding it. As usual, other people drifted to the scene. The trial court would know them as: thirty-seven-year-old drug addict, Robert Neinberg; twenty-three-year-old alcoholic, Doug Mull; and twenty-two-year-old Shirley Baker.

At nine o'clock, Hope and Doug Mull left to visit the Ottawa fair. Before leaving, Hope asked Candy to watch her daughter, Cynthia, who was playing at the foot of the breezeway steps. She told Candy that Cynthia needed a bath and asked her to bathe her. She added that she had already left clean pyjamas out for Cynthia to wear. Candy agreed to do what Hope had asked her to do.

Between ten and ten-thirty, Robert Neinberg, Candy and

Kenny left the shindig and drove less than a mile to the town centre on an alcohol run. They found the convenience store in Columbus Grove closed so they drove four miles to a store in Ottawa. Between eleven and eleven-thirty, they returned with whisky, cheap wine and a case of beer. By that time, everyone had converged in Peggy's apartment.

Cynthia had been bathed and put to bed at nine-thirty and left alone as usual. Peggy's two children were also in their beds and Shirley Baker was looking after Jason, Candy's son.

Minutes after returning from the booze run, Mike Nichols approached Kenny. Mike knew of Candy and Kenny's prior relationship and he became confused when he observed them leaving together on the booze run, reading into it more than there was.

'I'd like to talk to you outside, OK?' he said.

Kenny agreed. 'I'll be out in a minute,' he said. His words were slurred. He finished his drink and left Peggy's.

He descended the breezeway steps and found Mike by the tool shed in front of Candy's apartment. Mike asked him if he was still involved with Candy.

Kenny shook his head. 'Nah, no way. Why?'

'Because, you know, I got me, you know, very strong feelings for her.'

Kenny shrugged. 'She's all yours, pal.'

At this point, Candy appeared whereupon Mike hunched his shoulders and scowled at Kenny.

Kenny caught the hostile exchange and said, 'Don't try to act like a hard man to show off to your girlfriend here. Broken hand or no', I'll knock ye on your arse.'

Apparently believing they were arguing over her, Candy stepped to Mike's side and placed her hand on his arm, saying she would rather be with him. Kenny and Mike ignored her. Mike didn't respond to Kenny's threat verbally. Instead, he stuck out his chest, appearing combative.

Kenny called his bluff. 'Alright, that's it, let's go – you and me, come on.'

Mike's tough guy act crumbled as he retreated a step. 'I don't want no trouble.'

'Then quit acting like ye want to kick my head in.'

Mike shook his head. 'I'm a lover, not a fighter.'

Kenny chuckled. 'Aye, OK, Casanova.'

In a later newspaper interview, Mike Nichols said that Kenny then shook his hand, wished him good luck and walked off to go up the breezeway steps to Peggy's.

Although the confrontation was presented some months later at Kenny's murder trial by the prosecution to support the proposed motive that Kenny was so angry with Mike and Candy that he attempted to kill them, Kenny's subsequent behaviour contradicted this. In Peggy's apartment, he shared a half bottle of whisky with Mike – hardly the kind of gesture that a man who harboured ill feelings towards someone might make.

At approximately midnight, Doug, Robert and Hope entered Hope's apartment. Hope and Doug had returned from Ottawa with hashish and they began smoking from a pipe. Around half an hour later, further establishing that Kenny held no grudge towards Mike, they went in to Hope's apartment together and both took a couple of hits from the pipe. As Hope would attest at trial, 'They seemed to be getting along real well.'

Mike and Kenny returned to Peggy's after a few minutes and Mike warmed the sofa next to Candy. They began kissing and petting. Kenny got another drink and knelt on the floor next to the stereo, facing Peggy, Bob and Shirley, who was holding Candy's child. They drank and talked above the music. A catchy song of the day played on the stereo – 'Burning Down the House' by Talking Heads. It would prove ominous.

Peggy's brother, Jim, stepped into the apartment. He'd come from McDonald's and had a cheeseburger and fries. From Shirley's lap, one-year-old Jason motioned for something to eat.

Having already had a burger, Jim handed the child the food. In Peggy's words, 'Candy's boy just gobbled it right down. He was starving. She hadn't fed him for hours.'

Candy's negligence infuriated Peggy's boyfriend Bob, particularly because the boy was sitting in a soiled nappy. He said, 'Instead of sitting there and kissing all over Mike, why don't you take your little boy home and feed him and change his diaper? Shirley's been watching him all night long.' He sprung to his feet and stabbed a finger in her direction. 'You don't deserve your child because you're an unfit mother.'

Furious with Bob, Candy got up saying, 'I am not an unfit mother.' Her lower lip trembled and she broke into tears. Mike remained seated, his mouth hanging open. Composing herself, Candy said, 'C'mon Mike, let's go home.' and they did just that. After putting her son to bed, Candy led Mike to her bedroom. They had sex and then drifted off to sleep. When they awoke a few hours later, a life had already been lost.

Much of what evolved after Candy and Mike's departure remains unclear. Hope entered Peggy's apartment at around 1.40 a.m. Doug and Robert had gone home. Shirley swore she left Peggy's at 2.10 a.m. At 2.30 a.m., Hope returned to her apartment. Kenny left at around the same time, going on a drunken caper to take flowers from McAdam's Commercial Greenhouse across the road.

One of the most damaging things for Kenny was to be the allegation that he threatened to burn down A-building. Kenny has always denied making any such statement. Peggy would later testify that, at 2.20 a.m., while in the presence of Bob and Shirley, Kenny 'went into the kitchen and got a bottle of whisky and wine and said he was going to go row again, then he knelt down on the floor and he said, "Before the night is over, A-building is going to burn down."' Peggy claimed she asked him how he would do it and he allegedly said that he'd use his marine corps tactics whereupon Peggy replied, 'If you burn it down, don't burn down my apartment. I can't afford it.' Peggy testified that everybody heard him make the statement – specifically Bob and Shirley. Neither Bob nor Shirley confirmed this.

Shirley later testified that Kenny said, 'A-building is going to burn sometime or someday.' She claimed he made this remark around midnight, two-and-a-half hours before Peggy's assertion, adding that Hope had also been present. Hope testified that she never heard Kenny make such a threat. Bob testified that Peggy and a few other people were present when Kenny allegedly said he was going to '*blow up* A-building'. Bob claimed that Kenny made this statement between the hours of ten and midnight.

None of the three statements were the same and nor could the witnesses agree at what time the statements were made. But the statements from these witnesses would become the basis of the evidence that would lead to the first capital murder trial Putnam County had staged since the mid 1800s. Peggy Price, despite her testimony, would later admit that she had only told the assigned assistant prosecutor what he wanted to hear. In an interview for the respected television programme, *American Justice*, she would further admit that Kenny had not made a threat but had actually been singing along with the lyrics of the Talking Heads song, 'Burning Down the House'. Who would ever have thought that singing a song could end in the destruction of a man's life?

After leaving Peggy's apartment at 2.30 a.m., Kenny staggered to McAdam's Commercial Greenhouse. During the drunken mischief, he pinched two plotted plants 'for a laugh'. As he later explained, we all do some stupid things when we're young and drunk.

On hearing noises coming from the greenhouse, Hope, who had been eating a snack, stepped out on to her balcony. She saw Kenny on the pavement in front of A-building. 'What're you doing, Scotty?' she said, calling him by the name many Scots acquire in America.

He shrugged. 'Nothing much. Can I come up?'

Hope nodded. He then climbed the steps and went in to her apartment. The time was approximately 2.45 a.m. It was a humid night and they just stood on her balcony talking.

At 3.15 a.m. or thereabout, a customised old Ford pick-up truck pulled alongside the south-side kerb that faced A-building. One of Hope's drug dealers, Dennis Smith, was driving. His friend, Todd Ellerbrook, was slouched in the passenger seat. Upon seeing the truck, Hope, followed by Kenny, left the apartment.

Hope later testified that Kenny leaned on the passenger-side door while she leaned against the driver's-side door and talked to Dennis. Dennis asked her if she wanted to go set off fireworks at his place. Hope claimed that she told him that she had no babysitter and that Kenny volunteered by saying, 'Well, I'll keep an eye on her if you'll let me sleep on your couch.'

Hope testified that Dennis leaned forward to Kenny and said, 'Are you sure you don't mind?' to which Kenny allegedly replied, 'No.' Hope then attested that she returned to her apartment for a long-sleeved shirt. A minute later, she squeezed into the truck between Dennis and Todd. Before Dennis pulled away, Hope claimed that she observed Kenny and later testified, 'I'm *pretty* sure I seen him going up the steps and up to the front door.' Then she said, 'I *think* I saw him open the front door to go in.'

Ten minutes later, she said she arrived at Dennis Smith's house and there they drank some more and shot off some fireworks. At approximately 4.30 a.m., she and Dennis went to bed together.

Her memory of events are suspect. Neither of the two men in the truck, nor a woman, Donna Michaels, who viewed the scene from her bedroom window, corroborated Hope's testimony. It would be understandable if she had made some degree of error – few people can recall their every step – but her testimony was so far from that of the three others that she must have invented her story. Her motive for doing so? Perhaps she wanted to shift the responsibility of the welfare of her child to Kenny.

According to Kenny, Dennis, Todd and Donna Michaels, Kenny never leaned on the truck – he never even approached the vehicle. He stood on the pavement halfway between the truck and the apartment building. Hope leaned against the passenger door for a few minutes, talking, before, finally, Dennis said, 'If you're going with us, get your fucking ass in here.'

'Just a minute,' she replied and she returned to her apartment to put some shoes on her feet and probably, as she did indeed testify, pull on a long-sleeved shirt.

Just before she climbed into the truck, she faced Kenny and called out to him, 'Scotty, go upstairs and look after Scootie (Cynthia's nickname) – she's asleep.'

In no condition to babysit, Kenny shook his head, saying, 'Nah, uh-uh.'

Having already fetched the shoes and shirt, Hope apparently decided to leave regardless of whether or not she had a babysitter – after all, she often left her child alone.

Donna Michaels had been woken up by the noise of the souped-up truck engine and, although she heard Hope tell Kenny to go upstairs and look after Cynthia, she did not hear Kenny's response. Dennis and Todd didn't even hear Hope telling Kenny to babysit. In fact, Dennis testified that Hope told him that she was going to ask Mike to babysit. Mike denied that she asked him.

In any case, contrary to Hope's claim, Kenny made no move to enter her apartment. As the truck pulled away, he remained standing on the pavement. Donna Michaels confirmed this. Just after the truck disappeared, Donna attested that she saw Kenny leave the path, stagger a few feet across the grass and collapse in a clump of bushes. About five minutes passed and, just when Donna considered getting dressed to go and check on Kenny's condition, he stirred, got up and wobbled on to his feet. He staggered on to the path and headed through the breezeway. At that point, he disappeared from Donna's sight – the time was approximately 3.35 a.m.

Kenny claims he walked back to our dad's house. Inside the apartment, he drank some hot chocolate and decided to go to bed. But, when he lay down, the ceiling began to spin and he felt sick. So he got up and smoked a cigarette. His relationship with our father had been holding by threads and the last thing he wanted to do was provoke Dad who slept in the adjacent thin-walled room. He lay on the bed again and still the ceiling spun – a prelude to him throwing up. The bathroom stood facing our dad's bedroom door and he didn't dare throw up in there for fear of waking him. He got up and left the apartment, intending to spend the night in Dad's car.

As he approached the parking lot, he heard sirens and saw flashing lights nearing the apartment complex. His attention was drawn to A-building. Smoke billowed from the roof. He broke into a run and turned on to the path along the side of B-building. He passed a resident, Sandra Spencer, and her four sleepy-eyed children. They were the first people to see Kenny since he had gone out of Donna Michaels' sight fifty minutes before. The time was approximately 4.25 a.m. No one can corroborate Kenny's story about what he was doing during this fifty-minute period – only he knows the truth.

Kenny is a liar, according to Assistant Prosecutor Randall Basinger. He alleges that Kenny did not walk home, as he claimed, but set about his murderous deed.

5

NO SMOKE WITHOUT FIRE

When Kenny stepped out of Donna Michaels' view, Assistant Prosecutor Basinger asserted, he never passed through the breezeway heading for home. Instead, he procured fire accelerants – petrol and paint thinner. Basinger claimed Kenny stole these accelerants from McAdam's Commercial Greenhouse – the same place where he'd trespassed and stolen the plants.

After procuring cans of petrol and paint thinner, Kenny returned to A-building, to the tool shed that squatted below Hope Collins's balcony. He wore military camouflage, 'which he would want to wear for such an occasion,' asserted Basinger.

The State fire marshal's theory, which the prosecution relied on, alleged that Kenny placed the cans of accelerants – his weapons of murder – on to the sloping roof of the tool shed and then, as silently as a cat burglar, he climbed on to the top of the shed. Eight feet away glistened the reflection of a streetlight against a window. Behind the glass of that open window, lay Candy Barchet and Mike Nichols together in bed. These two were Kenny's intended targets.

From the roof of the shed, Kenny supposedly heaved the cans of accelerants up and deposited them on the deck of Hope's balcony, which was some four feet higher than the shed rooftop. Then he stealthily climbed on to the balcony, slid open the glass door and stepped into the living room of Hope Collins's apartment. According to Basinger, a 'hedonistic, sociopathic rage' consumed Kenny. After disconnecting the smoke detector, he poured the petrol and paint thinner 'through the living room of that apartment and ignited those accelerants in an attempt to kill Mike Nichols and in an attempt to kill Candy Barchet in the apartment immediately below.'

'The reason?' Basinger would ask the court. 'To get back at his girlfriend's lover – a girlfriend that he had been seeing for the past two weeks, had been going to bed with himself and who was in fact immediately below with someone else. The result? He killed two-year-old Cynthia Collins who was in the apartment, who he knew was in the apartment. This man,' Basinger would say, directing a finger at Kenny across the courtroom, 'this man with his purpose to murder two people down below, ended up murdering two-year-old Cynthia Collins.'

After setting the fire, Kenny had allegedly made his escape back over the balcony with the empty accelerant cans, moving as silently as had when he had climbed up. He then disappeared from the scene, only to return later when Sandra Spencer and her children witnessed him running toward the fire.

6

ACCUSED

Minutes after Kenny had left the apartment, Dad woke to the sound of a mother consoling a crying child as they passed his bedroom window. The reflection of coloured emergency lights bounced off the bedroom walls. Dad threw back his sheet and jumped from the bed. He smudged the glass as he peered through the window and looked out over the apartment complex's grassy field. Two police cars were parked on the road that crossed in front of A-building.

'Kenny!' he called. On receiving no answer, he became alarmed. He pulled on his trousers, slid into his slippers and snatched his bathrobe before rushing from the apartment.

Smoke filled the air and it grew thicker as he strode the length of B-building. As he rounded A-building, he saw smoke funnelling from an upper apartment. A fire truck sat by the kerb, its hoses spilled like intestines over the pavement. A fire team untwisted the hoses and battled to connect them to a nearby fire hydrant. Near the truck, a congregation of people dressed in nightclothes stared at the smoking apartment. Dad approached the crowd and, as he got nearer to the apartment, he spotted two figures struggling on the upper breezeway. 'Oh God,' he blurted.

One of the figures was Kenny and the other was a fireman. Kenny tried to break the fireman's grip and enter the furnace.

Repeatedly, he yelled, 'There's a kid in there – let me go – there's a kid in there.' His words were slurred. A deputy ascended the breezeway to assist in Kenny's removal but still Kenny resisted.

'Drunk and making a damn nuisance of himself,' Dad mumbled. Embarrassed by the scene, he returned to his apartment.

Rejecting the urge to go back to bed, he showered and then made coffee. As he settled into his comforter, hot cup in hand, someone knocked on the door. When he answered it, he faced his friend and neighbour, Scott Tice. As he stepped through the door, Scott asked Dad if he knew what was going on.

'Only that there's been a fire up front and Kenny was getting in the way and making a spectacle of himself.'

'I'm afraid there's more to it than that,' Scott replied. He then told Dad that Cynthia Collins had died in the fire and people were accusing Kenny of starting it.

Feeling weak in the legs, Dad lowered himself to the couch. He reached for a cigarette on the coffee table. He asked if anyone saw Kenny start the fire.

'Not that I'm aware of. The story is that he told someone at a party he was going to burn up the building.'

Dad lowered his head, squeezing his eyes. 'Do the police know?'

'I don't know but he's in their custody now.'

Dad began to cry. The next thing he remembers is opening his eyes minutes later to an empty, silent room.

At approximately 6.45 a.m., Kenny stepped into the apartment, breaking that silence.

Gilbert Michaels, Donna Michaels' husband, had arrived at the burning apartment first. He flung open the screen door but, as soon as he opened the metal front door, it was similar to opening the hatch to a furnace and the escaping heat pushed him back. As he would later testify, 'It was throwing sparks and everything right out at me. There was no way I could get in.'

When Kenny rushed up the stair and on to the breezeway, he hopped from foot to foot, visibly frustrated. He groaned, 'There's a baby inside.'

Gilbert Michaels shook his head. 'There's no way I can get in there.' A moment later, he hopelessly turned to alert neighbours.

Kenny hesitated, clenched his jaw and then rushed forward, his legs pumping him into the burning apartment. As flames licked the walls and rolled across the ceiling, he was only able to take two or three steps before the heat sucked the air from his lungs, searing them and broiling his skin and singeing his hair. Thick black smoke swirled around him like dark curtains. Cinders popped before his blurred and stinging eyes. The room crackled like breakfast cereal. He back-pedalled out of the apartment.

He made three more attempts but, each time, the wall of heat repelled him. Don Hoyt, one of the first firefighters on the scene, later swore, 'I saw someone come out of the door of the apartment on fire. I helped him up and he wanted to go back in.'

Fireman Hoyt would testify that Kenny began screaming about Cynthia being in the apartment, yelling, 'She's in there.' Hoyt restrained Kenny from entering again. Asked if Kenny's actions constituted that of a person showing complete disregard for his own safety, Hoyt stated, 'Yes. Going into that apartment without equipment on – yes.'

A young Scot might have been hailed a hero for his desperate attempts to fight his way through flames to save the life of a little girl – instead, he was accused of her murder.

After his struggle with the fireman, a deputy sheriff, joined by another, removed Kenny from the breezeway landing. Kenny continued to struggle, hysterically clamouring at them to let him go. 'There's a little girl in the flat,' he shouted.

He managed to break free but the deputies blocked his way from charging back up the breezeway steps. He moved into a combative stance, threatening them if they didn't get out of his way. At that time, Columbus Grove Police Chief, Thomas Miller, appeared from the confusion – a deputy, realising the seriousness of the situation, had requested the chief's assistance.

Dressed in civilian clothes, the chief stepped in front of Kenny. 'C'mon, son – come with me,' he said coolly, beckoning Kenny with a wave of his hand. Kenny paused and then physically relaxed. He followed the police chief to a cruiser that was parked a short distance away from all the activity.

As the police chief later testified, he placed Kenny in the rear of his cruiser and locked him in the back. His reason for doing so was to prevent Kenny from rejoining the fire scene. The chief sat in the front of the car and offered Kenny a cigarette through the screened partition. They smoked and talked. Kenny informed him that Hope had left earlier. 'Her kid is still in the apartment.'

The chief would swear that Kenny was 'real concerned about the fire and the child' and he agreed that Kenny appeared emotionally distraught and agitated. Asked to recall if he could render an opinion regarding Kenny's alcohol consumption, the chief would state, 'Oh, yes, he had alcohol on his breath heavy.' And, when asked if was he was able to detect the smell of paint thinner or petrol on Kenny, the police chief stated, 'No.'

When a firefighter dressed in protective gear carried the seemingly sleeping body of Cynthia from the apartment, the emergency medical services (EMS) personnel took her and rushed her to the ambulance. They tried unsuccessfully to resuscitate her. Only one burn scarred Cynthia's body – a circular first-degree one, an inch in diameter, on her left wrist. Most believed a hot door handle caused it but logic would cast doubt on this theory.

Chief Miller ordered one of his deputies to stay by his cruiser while he left. He walked to the EMS vehicle then returned a couple of minutes later, having been unable to discover Cynthia's condition because there had been too much activity. Relieving his deputy, the chief again sat in the cruiser. After a short time (at around 6.00 a.m.), being powerless to do anything more at the scene, he started the cruiser and pulled from the kerb with Kenny still in the back seat. Within minutes, they parked in front of the small Columbus Grove Police Department building. The chief stepped out and opened the door for Kenny.

The chief ushered Kenny into his office and asked him if he could answer a few questions so that a report could be compiled. Kenny answered little more than a half-dozen questions dealing with the whereabouts of Hope Collins, what time he arrived at the fire, what he observed upon arriving etc. At exactly 6.27 a.m., he stopped questioning Kenny and noted the time on the voluntary statement form. Miller signed the form and then handed the pen to Kenny. Kenny placed the pen in his right hand, his broken hand, and signed his full signature to the form – 'Kenneth T. Richey'. It would become an important point later.

The chief warned Kenny that, when he returned to the apartment complex, he had to stay away from the fire scene. Kenny agreed. A moment later, they left the station and returned to the flats. The time was approximately 6.45 a.m. On arriving back at the scene, the police chief spoke with deputies and fire personnel. When he learned of Cynthia's death, Miller called the State fire investigator's office to clarify State procedure. He was told that, if death resulted from a fire, a State fire marshal had to conduct an investigation into the fire's cause. Within minutes of the call to the fire investigator's office, sixty-three-year-old Fire Marshal Robert Cryer travelled from the town of Defiance, a one-hour drive from Columbus Grove, to conduct his investigation of the fire. It was just another one of thousands of fires the fire marshal had been called to investigate during his twelve years' service as a State fire investigator.

Chief Miller did not call the fire investigator's office until around 6.55 a.m., meaning that the fire marshal could not have possibly arrived at the complex before 7.55 a.m. But the fire marshal would testify he reached the scene at 6.45 a.m. – before Chief Miller had even called. This was not to be the fire marshal's only inconsistency.

The first investigation of the fire was conducted by Columbus Grove Fire Chief, Len Hefner, a respected 'fire expert'. He concluded that the fire had started 'electrically'. The evidence shows that, after arriving at the scene, the fire marshal concurred with this opinion.

At Kenny's trial, the apartment complex manager, Sherry Tice, stated that she had been standing in the complex's laundry room when the State fire marshal entered. Cecil Steigle, the owner of the apartment complex, stepped out of the manager's office and met with the fire marshal for the second time that morning. Sherry Tice heard the fire marshal inform Cecil Steigle that the fire had been caused by a portable fan that had tipped over and shorted out.

In an affidavit obtained from Peggy Price, three months after Kenny's trial, Peggy swore, 'Just after the fire in apartment A-13, I asked the fire marshal to check my smoke alarm when he came into my apartment for water damage. He told me not to use the electricity because he thought the fire was caused by electricity and the wires were wet from the fire.'

However, at trial, the fire marshal would testify, 'At the scene, I did not feel that the fan had anything to do with the fire.' The fire marshal also stated that he came to the conclusion that, on June the thirtieth, the day of the fire, it was a 'suspicious fire', adding, 'I never state a fire is arson until I get my lab reports back.'

At trial, Kenny's court-appointed attorney, William Kluge,

would ask Fire Marshal Cryer, 'Had you told anyone earlier that day, on June thirtieth, that you believed the fire to be caused by the fan?'

'No,' Cryer replied.

'You never made that statement?' Attorney Kluge countered.

'Well, there was people around there saying the fan and I said, "Well, I don't think so." And then, after I looked at it and got to it, I said, "I don't think the fan had anything to do with the fire because, if the fan would have done it, it [the fire] would have been located right there and that would have been it." It wouldn't have been an intense fire.'

Cryer failed to elaborate who the 'people' were that he made his opinion known to and nor did anyone corroborate that they heard him offer such an opinion. In fact, his claims were contradicted by three people – Peggy Price, Sherry Tice and Cecil Steigle.

The evidence that conflicts with Cryer's position most was the fact that the apartment was completely gutted and cleaned after Cryer spoke to Cecil Steigle in the laundry room. The gutting of the apartment supports the claims of Cecil Steigle and Sherry Tice, who stated that the fire marshal concluded that the fire had been caused by a tipped fan because, in concluding that the fan caused the fire, there would be no further need to preserve the fire scene. On the other hand, if Fire Marshal Cryer had genuinely believed the fire's cause was 'suspicious', he would never have permitted the removal of burnt furnishings, especially the carpet, which had been dumped in the Putnam County landfill.

At trial, Kluge asked Cryer, 'Did you tell the police or anyone who was doing the investigation to save the carpet to see if they could test for accelerants?'

'Yes, yes, we saved the fire scene and kept it saved.'

Kluge parried, 'Well, how did the carpet get out at the dump then if you told them that?'

'The fellow that ran the motel or apartments came down from I believe it was Mansfield and he got all excited and kept pressuring and he up and cleaned it out, which we wasn't expecting him to clean that much. We were only expecting him to take the debris out and not clean the floors and walls and everything out of it.'

It is difficult to believe that, if Cryer considered the fire suspicious in nature, he would allow one impatient individual to tamper with or interfere with a potential crime scene, by ruining or destroying evidence. Fire investigation procedures dictate that potential arson scenes be secured and cordoned off to prohibit unauthorised personnel from disturbing evidence.

The complex owner, Cecil Steigle, denied ever pressuring Cryer to allow the cleaning of the apartment. After Cryer informed Cecil Steigle that the fan caused the fire, Steigle asserts that the fire marshal told him he could clean the entire apartment. Cryer made no stipulation to save the carpet or any other debris.

At Kenny's preliminary trial, the fire marshal testified that he spent all day, until 7.00 p.m., at the scene investigating the fire and then returned for most of the next day. Yet, what could he have been investigating? The apartment had been completely cleaned by Cecil Steigle.

Furthermore, if the fire marshal had been at the scene all day, then how could he have been ignorant of the apartment being gutted of all its contents and those contents being transported to the county dump? How could he not have seen the walls and floors being cleaned? Such a job would have taken several hours to do. If Cryer had been at the scene all day, as he testified he was, then he knew about the apartment being gutted and cleaned. He knew this, as evidence shows, because he did, in fact, give Cecil Steigle permission to gut the apartment after he had told him that the fan caused the fire. Also, not one fireman or policeman confirmed Cryer's claim that he had instructed them to save the carpet. The very fact that the carpet ended up in the county dump seems fair proof that no such instructions were given.

Yet, if Fire Marshal Cryer did not promulgate the arson theory, where did it come from?

Only after the fire marshal and Assistant Prosecutor Randall Basinger convened on July the first, the day after the fire, did the fire marshal suddenly begin to pursue an arson theory. On the stand, Cryer stated that he came to the conclusion on the afternoon of July the first that the fire was 'definitely' caused by arson. Following this, he stated that he authorised Basinger to bring arson charges against Kenny. He said this despite also declaring, 'I *never* state a fire is arson until I get my lab reports back.' It would be seventeen days after the fire before he even took a single sample for sending to the lab.

It is evident that Basinger actually spearheaded the arson investigation with Cryer being little more than a spectator. Supporting this is the fact that Basinger ordered items to be retrieved from the county dump for testing – namely, the fan and the carpet. The clothing Kenny had worn on the night of the fire was confiscated. What motivated Basinger to direct the investigation and what did he say to persuade Cryer to change his mind over what he had previously stated to be the cause of the fire? Was it possibly the allegation that Kenny threatened to burn A-building?

Shortly after the fire, Peggy Price told her cousin, a deputy sheriff, that she thought she heard Kenny make the threat. Word quickly spread through the apartment complex. One ear in particular took interest. That ear belonged to seventy-one-year-old Juanita Altimus, an A-building resident. She would become one of the State's key witnesses.

When Basinger learned of Kenny's alleged threat, probably on July the first, it provided him with the foundation on which to build a case for arson and murder, which, as a capital offence, would assure Basinger plenty of publicity. State elections were to be held in November and Basinger was running as a candidate to become a State judge. Any favourable publicity he could garner from July through to November could only improve his chances of winning the election. Moreover, it didn't hurt Basinger that the majority of the residents of the apartment complex had convicted and sentenced Kenny even before a formal murder charge was filed against him.

According to Police Chief Miller, when he and Sergeant Steve Stechschulte stepped into our father's apartment at noon on June the thirtieth, Kenny appeared to have a hangover. After returning to the house at approximately 6.45 a.m., Kenny had collapsed into a slumber on the living room sofa. Dad shook him awake when the two cops had come in and he stumbled to the bathroom. On his return, they sat at the dining room table. Chief Miller had assigned the investigation of the case to Sergeant Stechschulte of the Putnam County Sheriff's Department and the chief was really no more than an observer.

At this stage, they were seeking a suspect for 'child endangering' and 'involuntary manslaughter' charges. Those are the standard offences filed against anyone in Ohio State when a child dies through negligence while the care of the child is the responsibility of that person – the arson and murder investigation did not begin until the following afternoon, July the first.

Sticking to procedure, before asking Kenny questions, the sergeant advised him of his rights. Kenny acknowledged he understood and the sergeant noted this on a voluntary statement form. Once more, the sergeant advised Kenny that anything he said could later be used against him.

Kenny nodded. 'Go ahead, I'll talk. I've got nothing to hide.'

'OK,' the sergeant said, pen poised above the statement form. 'Can you tell me what you did from 6.00 p.m. last evening until the time of the fire at Hope Collins's residence?'

Kenny shrugged. 'I was on the landing by Hope's apartment

and we were partying – then I went home.'

'I see,' Stechschulte said, writing his questions and Kenny's answers word for word. 'And did Hope stay at the party the entire time?'

'No, not the entire time. She left and went to Denny's house or something.'

'Did Hope leave the apartment with some guys? If so, who?'

'Yes. I don't know who it was. He was bald in front, wore glasses and drove a black Cougar,' Kenny said, describing Doug Mull who left with Hope at nine o'clock during the party.

Stechschulte eyed Miller quizzically as if he was unsure of the man being described. Miller nodded. Stechschulte redirected his attention to Kenny. 'Did Hope ask you to babysit before she left?'

'No, but Candy Barchet told us she was taking care of Cynthia and she was going to get paid for it . . .'

'Wait a minute. You said Candy's last name is Barchet?'

Kenny nodded.

Stechschulte shook his head. 'I made a mistake. I wrote Johnson. Where that came from, I don't know.' He scratched four lines across the name, 'Johnson' and handed Kenny his pen. 'I need you to initial above the mistake.'

Kenny took the pen between the fingers of his broken hand and he initialled the change – 'KTR'.

Resuming the questioning, Stechschulte said, 'Did you, at any time, take care of Cynthia?'

'No, but I did check on her once. She was sleeping in her room or her mum's. I'm not sure which – I was really drunk.'

'OK, now let's shift on some – how did you find out about the fire?'

'I went over when I heard the sirens and saw the lights.'

'What did you do when you got to the apartment?'

'I tried to get in but I didn't get far because of the heat and the smoke.'

'And after that?'

'A police officer took me downstairs.'

'I see.' Stechschulte paused, pursing his lips – the detective mind at work. 'Let's switch some. When Hope left the apartments, did you go to the truck she got in?'

'No.'

'OK and, during the party, did you stay in Peggy's the entire time or did you walk in and out of her apartment?'

'No, we were partying outside the apartment and then went to Peggy's apartment. We were in Hope's apartment for a few minutes before going back to Peggy's.'

'Uh, hmm, I understand,' Stechschulte said, biting the end of his pen. 'OK, let's go back to Hope. Did she leave Cynthia in the apartment by herself often?'

'Sometimes.'

'Has she ever asked you, at anytime, to watch Cynthia?'

'No, she usually asks Peggy,' Kenny replied, not thinking to mention that she 'told' him to watch Cynthia that morning.

Wrapping up the questioning, Stechschulte sighed. 'Well, that's about it for now. Is there anything you'd like to add?'

Kenny shrugged. 'No, not really.'

Before leaving, Stechschulte, who had used three statement forms during the questioning, dated and witnessed each form, noting the time he completed the questioning – 1.23 p.m. The questioning had begun at 12.22 p.m. Kenny signed all three forms with his full signature. Before Miller and Stechschulte exited the apartment, Stechschulte told Kenny to stay home the following afternoon because he intended to return and ask him more questions.

Something, maybe the baritone of his voice, alarmed our dad. He sensed they planned to arrest Kenny the next day. He shared his fear with Kenny, who dismissed it with a shake of his head. 'Arrest me for what?'

He should have listened to a parent's intuition.

At 8.50 a.m. the next morning, Dad drove Kenny to St Rita's Medical Center in Lima to keep Kenny's appointment to have the cast on his arm changed. About an hour after the appointment they ate lunch at a Dairy Queen fast-food and ice-cream stop. After lunch, they stopped at a convenience store where there was an informal bar at the rear of the building. They had a beer and talked. Dad had had a bad dream the night before and he shared it with Kenny. The dream ended with Kenny in prison. It strengthened the brooding feeling that had followed him that morning, occasionally tapping his shoulder lest he forget its presence.

The time passed quickly and they drove back to the apartments at one-thirty. They agreed that, after dropping Kenny off, our dad would drive to Ottawa, where he would worry the afternoon away with some friends. If the police arrested Kenny, Dad said he would not be able to bear witnessing it. Before Kenny stepped from the car, Dad impulsively reached for him, hugging him tightly. He then watched Kenny walk away. The bright sun played off his hair like the shine of a new copper penny. Dad remembered thinking how it seemed like only yesterday that he sat in his car with our mum, watching Kenny walk hesitantly towards the gates of Sighthill Primary School in Edinburgh. He started the car as Kenny turned into the building and went out of sight. It was the last time Dad saw Kenny a free man.

The warrant for Kenny's arrest stemmed from a phone call from Hope Collins that the prosecutor's office received at 9.15 a.m. on July the first. Hope said she wished to pursue criminal charges against Kenny. This phone call occurred only after police had interviewed Hope. During the interview, the police notified her that she was facing child endangerment and involuntary manslaughter charges. In her phone call, she claimed that Kenny had said he would watch Cynthia.

Yet, if that was true, why did Hope wait so long to contact

the authorities? Why didn't she say something to the deputy who drove to Dennis Smith's house to inform her of Cynthia's death? If your child was in the custody and care of another person and something happened to your child, wouldn't you first ask, 'How can that be? The babysitter was watching her. What happened to the babysitter? He was supposed to be taking care of her?' Wouldn't that be every parent's natural reaction? Wasn't it odd to allow a full day to pass without saying a thing to anyone?

It was now apparent to Hope that the investigators were keen to find a person responsible for Cynthia's death through negligence and she directed her finger at Kenny. Despite Hope's attempt to deflect attention away from herself, Basinger, seemingly unimpressed by Hope's lack of emotion concerning the death of her child, filed child endangerment and involuntary manslaughter charges against her too. Deputies arrested her following Cynthia's funeral on July the sixth. She would spend forty-five days in jail before she agreed to a plea bargain – she would plead guilty to negligence by leaving Cynthia and, in return, would name Kenny as the person she'd left in charge of the little girl. As a result of her plea bargain, she received three years probation with credit for the time she'd already served.

Deputy Roy Sargent and Sergeant Stechschulte arrested Kenny at around two o'clock in the afternoon of July the first for child endangerment and involuntary manslaughter. Stech-schulte handcuffed him while reading the rights under their Miranda duty. Before leaving the apartment, Kenny shook his head in disbelief, saying, 'This is great for my dad – one son charged with murder and now this.' Looking very pale, he plodded from the apartment to a waiting police cruiser.

Behind him, he left a breeding ground of gossip that generated so many tales. One story was that he had supposedly sexually molested Cynthia and then deliberately started the fire to destroy the evidence of his dirty deed. Of course, autopsy reports stamped out this rumour but such gossip, although false, still had a negative effect.

He rode in silence to the Putnam County Sheriff's Department in Ottawa, which also housed the county jail. There, Deputy Sargent removed the handcuffs and escorted Kenny to an upper office in the two-storey building. Stechschulte took a seat behind a desk that faced the chair Kenny had lowered himself into and Deputy Sargent sat behind a desk to Kenny's right. From this point forward, Kenny felt ambushed – as if the authorities had set their crosshairs on him and were determined to bring him down no matter what it took, even if it meant bending a few rules to achieve their goal.

Once Stechschulte, Sargent and Kenny were seated, Stechschulte told Kenny he wanted to ask him some questions. At about this time, in another part of the county, at Basinger's instructions, two deputies pulled part of a charred chair and the carpet belonging to Hope Collins from underneath a pile of rubbish at the landfill. Fire Marshal Cryer would testify he knew nothing of the whereabouts of the carpet until July the twenty-first, some three weeks after the fire. It contradicts his claim that he instructed Basinger to retrieve the carpet.

Kenny refused to answer Stechschulte's questions and he requested a lawyer. Several times over the next couple of hours, he requested a lawyer and, in being denied one upon request, his basic rights were violated. Stechschulte told Kenny that an attorney would be provided for him at his arraignment hearing in a few days. 'Besides, you don't really need one right now anyway. We only want to ask a few questions. We think you can help us.' After a pause, Kenny agreed. At this point, his rights – or an agreement to a waiver of them – should have been read to him. They were not.

Stechschulte began to ask questions similar to those he'd asked the day before. He was killing time. Around an hour later, the office door opened and Assistant Prosecutor Basinger entered, followed by the State fire marshal, Robert Cryer. Kenny immediately recognised the sharp face of the man who had prosecuted him over the assault charge three years before. More recently, he'd seen his picture in the local newspaper. It was accompanied by an article that declared Basinger was a candidate for the post of judge in the county elections.

Stechschulte stood up, offered Basinger his chair and then left the office. Deputy Sargent also rose but he remained standing in the room as Cryer took his vacated seat. Basinger cleared his throat, loosening his wide tie that matched the wide lapels of his sport coat. 'How are you doing, Kenneth?'

'How do ye think I'm doing?' Kenny said, feeling as if the room was closing in on him.

Basinger spread his palms over the desk. 'I understand, I really do,' he said in an overly commiserating tone. Again he cleared his throat. 'My name is Randall Basinger. I'm the assistant prosecutor. I have some questions I'd like to ask you.'

The fire marshal then introduced himself and said, 'Listen, before we take your statements, do I have permission to record them? It will be much easier than writing it down.'

In no hurry to step into a jail cell, Kenny said, 'Ye can write things down but ye can't tape them.'

Despite Kenny's refusal to have his statements taped, the fire marshal secretly turned on his tape recorder about ten minutes into the questioning adding another inconsistency to the case which would become known as *The State of Ohio v. Kenneth Thomas Richey*. At Kenny's preliminary trial, Cryer refuted Kenny's statement that he hadn't wanted the interview taped. The fire marshal swore, 'Oh, we took the tape recorder and set it up and started the tape and the tape ran clear through the interview.' Asked if all present were certain the interview was going to be taped, Cryer testified, 'Yes.'

However, when questioned at the preliminary trial, Deputy Sargent testified that he had never seen any tape recorder and he didn't know that the fire marshal had turned on a tape recorder. Because Kluge intended to call Deputy Sargent to testify to the fact that he knew nothing of Cryer's tape recorder, thereby disputing Cryer's claims, Basinger asked for permission to approach the bench. Following a private discussion with the judge and Kluge, Basinger admitted the following:

> I have disclosed two matters which I feel the defence is entitled to know and one is that, in prior interviews with Fire Marshal Cryer, it was my understanding and my notes reflect that Robert Cryer indicated at the conclusion of the tape and before subsequent statements that Kenneth Richey did make a statement that he wanted to talk with an attorney. It is also my understanding that there will be testimony concerning whether or not Kenneth Richey consented to the tape recording which, in effect, testimony will, it's my understanding, show that Kenneth Richey did not consent to that the tape recording and I don't know whether Robert Cryer heard these statements but there was some discussion and the defendant, Kenneth Richey, stated he did not consent but it was turned on anyway.

It is impossible to believe that Fire Marshal Cryer did not hear Kenny's refusal to be taped. In fact, Cryer testified that, upon asking for his permission to be taped, Kenny responded, 'It's all right with me.' Questioned another time regarding the subject, Cryer stated that Kenny answered, 'Well, that's all right – use the tape recorder.'

If Cryer would seemingly lie in open court about a tape recorder, how many other instances in this case did his apparent dishonesty guide his conduct? It's a wonder that he could attain such a position of professional authority. More troubling is the fact that, in Cryer's twelve years as a fire marshal, his testimony contributed to the convictions of dozens of people.

Another matter that came into dispute was whether Kenny's rights were read to him, as required by law, prior to the questioning. Kenny denies that they were. 'If they were, they would have had to allow me an attorney like I requested,' he said of the time.

A Waiver of Rights form, presented at the preliminary trial, stated that the suspect had been advised of his rights and chose to waive them in order to speak voluntarily. Deputy Sargent's signature appears at the foot of the form as a witness and Kenny's initials appear where his signature should be. It is initialled with a child-like squiggly 'KR'. This document, Kenny claims, is a forgery. Questioned regarding the reason for the squiggly initials, Fire Marshal Cryer testified, 'Well, Kenneth had his hand in a cast and he couldn't write so he just signed his initials to it.' The irony of this, of course, was that the prosecution wanted the court to believe that his hand was too disabled to hold a pen properly yet it was strong enough to carry two cans of accelerants, climb up on to a shed roof with them, hoist them over a balcony and then climb back down again.

The evidence supporting Kenny's claim that the Waiver of Rights form was a forgery is convincing. Kenny's short question and answer statement taken by Chief Miller following the fire was signed with Kenny's full signature. All three statement forms from his questioning by Stechschulte were also signed in full. Also, Kenny's claim that he never initials anything with only his first and last initials is substantiated by examples of forms from his military file where, in the military, the act of initialling is common practice. All forms are initialled 'KTR'. Finally, during the questioning session the previous afternoon, Stechschulte had made a written mistake. He'd crossed out his error, the name 'Johnson', with four lines and he had got Kenny to initial above it to indicate that he agreed to the change. It is initialled, 'KTR'.

After the illegal taping of Kenny's interrogation, the prosecution got a transcript of it typed up using the tape because, although he had pretended to write down the questions and answers, the fire marshal hadn't actually bothered to do so. The prosecution tried to introduce the transcript they'd had typed to replace the taped version. It was the most obvious indication of the lengths Basinger would go to in order to railroad Kenny, to set him up to take a fall. However, the transcript had been blatantly doctored. There were examples of the deletion of words in Kenny's answers which made it appear that he had admitted to certain accusations when he'd actually denied them. The court threw the transcript out and, instead, they relied upon the taped version. Of course, this should also have been thrown out because Kenny never consented to the recording.

Not that it made a difference because Kenny had made no incriminating statement during the interrogation except for admitting that he'd unlawfully entered McAdam's Commercial Greenhouse to take a couple of plants just for kicks. For this, he was charged with breaking and entering. Apart from this incident, Kenny continually reasserted his innocence during the interrogation.

Basinger had begun by asking Kenny about his movements on the early evening of June the twenty-ninth – the night of the party. The tape hadn't been turned on until about ten minutes into the interrogation so the initial exchanges hadn't been captured. The first thing on the tape was when Basinger leaned forward and said, 'So, the first that you saw there was a fire was when?'

Kenny shrugged. 'When I saw the lights.' Kenny then established that he headed to the fire and tried entering the flat to save Cynthia.

A kitbag Kenny had left in Peggy's apartment on the morning of the twenty-ninth, containing his camping gear, was touched upon. Suspected to have been used to carry accelerant containers, the forensic lab later tested it but it they couldn't find the presence of any accelerants.

Kenny's history was brought up, including his assault conviction three years before.

'It was self-defence,' Kenny stated.

Basinger frowned. 'I think I handled that charge. You had O'Malley, I think?'

Kenny rolled his eyes and faced the fire marshal and the deputy. 'Yeah and it was wrong.' He pointed a finger at Basinger, scowling. 'He was a drinking buddy of his and, in a small town like this, someone like me doesn't stand a bloody chance.'

Basinger did not deny Kenny's accusation.

For the second time during the interrogation, Basinger asked about the fan. 'You don't remember if the fan was running?'

'I don't know if the fan was on or not.'

'But you do remember the fan?'

'What's the big thing with the fan?'

'Well,' Basinger said, 'we think, I don't know, the fan may have started the fire. I just wanted to know if Hope left it on or not?'

'I don't know if she did or not,' Kenny replied.

Basinger was then heard asking him about babysitting Cynthia.

'No,' Kenny replied. 'I never said I'd babysit. I will not babysit for a kid when I'm drunk.'

'Hope made the statement that she put you in charge.'

Kenny exploded. 'I don't know why she would say it but I'm telling ye now I wasn't babysitting and I'll be damned if I'm fucking charged with it. I'm going to take a polygraph test. I was not in charge of her kid and I'm not going to be arrested for it. She doesn't know what the hell she is talking about.'

'Well, I'm telling you that's what Hope's saying.'

'Well, I'm not the one responsible. I wasn't in charge of her kid. I'm not about to turn around and agree to babysit any child when I'm drunk.'

Basinger was then heard to inquire about his relationship with Candy and Kenny said he'd never had a serious relationship, a lasting relationship, with her.

'OK,' Basinger said, 'so it really wasn't working out with sex any more, was it?'

Kenny nodded. 'I got disgusted when, uh, when I found her with John Butler.'

'So you pretty much broke it off then?'

'Aye, you could say that but we were not really going together so we really couldn't break it off.'

'OK, but you stopped . . .'

'I stopped going to bed with her.'

'OK,' Basinger replied. He paused and could be heard drumming his fingers against the table. 'Do you remember making some threats or saying something was going to happen to Candy?'

'I wouldn't do anything to her.'

'So you never made any threats?'

He shook his head. 'I don't hit women. I never made any threats.'

'Well, not necessarily about hitting anybody. But did you ever make any threats about anything – about burning anything?'

'No.'

'Any idea why Peggy Price would say that if you didn't make the statement?'

'I don't know. My dad already told me someone over there had said that and I totally disagree with it because I know I damn well didn't.'

'OK,' Basinger said, 'do you remember saying anything about using your marine corps background?'

'Yes.'

'What did you say?'

'Something about, if they were going to be evicted, I'd blow the landlord's car up.'

'You'd blow the landlord's car up?'

'Not the one there now but the one who is going to be here in a week or something.' Kenny remembered making the comment but it had been tongue-in-cheek. 'I don't know who he is but he's supposed to be a real arsehole and he's going to kick Peggy and Hope out because of their bad reputations.'

'Do you remember saying that night to Peggy that you were going to use some of that marine corps background to get at Candy?'

Kenny could be heard sighing. 'Don't be daft.'

'You don't remember saying that?'

'I would never say that.'

As the tape of the interrogation wound down, Basinger could be heard asking Kenny about his bomb-making experience as he tried to make a connection between bombs and fires. Kenny had volunteered the truth, saying that he did know how to make a car bomb. From this line of questioning, Basinger was heard to ask, 'So you pretty much knew how to start a fire then if you wanted to?'

'The marines never taught us how to start fires – just how to blow things up.'

'OK, but do you think . . .'

'Look,' Kenny said, cutting in, 'when you see the enemy, you blow them up. You don't . . . fuck, ye know . . . set them on fire.'

Again, Basinger was heard asking if Kenny remembered saying anything about torching A-building.

And again Kenny was heard to disagree. 'I didn't say that.'

When Basinger had continued in the same vein, Kenny remembers throwing his hands up in exasperation. 'Now if I was going to torch the building, I sure as hell wouldn't tell anybody!' he was heard to say on the tape.

Basinger, a note of menace in this tone, retorted with, 'Unless you make it look like an accident.'

'Even in an accident – if I was to turn around and make it look like an accident right after I threatened to burn the place, who's going to get the blame still? Me.'

'Unless you were drunk and still did it anyway. Any reason why these people would say that if it weren't true?'

'No, I don't. I already told ye I'll take a polygraph.'

'C'mon, isn't it true, Ken?' Basinger said, lowering his voice.

Kenny's recalls his face reddening with frustration. 'I'm telling ye *no* – it isn't true,' he said.

'I'm asking you again?'

Sounding as though he was speaking through gritted teeth, he said, 'I wouldn't set fire to some building with kids in it.'

Then there was the sound of Basinger expelling a heavy breath. 'All right,' he said, 'you're denying making any statement remotely connecting that?'

'Perfectly true.'

'OK, is there anything you'd like to tell us, Ken?'

'Only that it wasn't me who started the fire and it wasn't me that was supposed to be babysitting.'

Concluding, Basinger said, 'Any more questions, anybody? You got any questions?' he asked Kenny.

'Aye. Am I being charged or what?'

'Yes.'

'Why?'

'Because you're being charged.'

'I need a phone call then.'

'OK, why don't you go with me?' Deputy Sargent said.

At this point the tape ended and Kenny remembers Sergent stepping around the desk and leading him out of the office. Kenny felt completely numb.

At Kenny's murder trial, regarding the interrogation, Basinger and the fire marshal claimed Kenny had repeatedly answered that he didn't know and that he'd been drinking heavily, making it sound like he had been evasive and dishonest. This is simply untrue. He answered questions in a forthright, even insistent, manner. Basinger would also claim that Kenny made conflicting statements on important points. This, also, is untrue. Not only did Basinger fail to disclose to the court the nature of these important conflicting points, they cannot be found in the taped interrogation. Indeed, although Kenny's taped statements were admissible in the grand jury proceedings, Basinger neglected to submit the tape. This was probably because Kenny made no statements that supported the serious charges Basinger was levelling against him.

After being booked for one count of child endangerment and one count of manslaughter, Kenny called Dad who, in turn, called our mum. Following that short, difficult telephone call to our dad, a jailer escorted him, dressed in orange overalls, to the empty cell that would be his home for nearly seven months.

Nine days later, on July the tenth, Basinger stood before a grand jury that consisted of a dozen of the town's people. He waved papers before their eyes – they contained Peggy Price's statement alleging that Kenny threatened to set fire to A-building. This evidence produced the charges of one count of aggravated arson and one count of aggravated murder. No physical evidence was presented to the grand jury. It would still be over two weeks before samples of evidence were tested.

With no physical evidence proving that arson had taken place, Basinger's case was weak. Unless some physical evidence was produced, he would be unable to win his case. Yet, at this point, producing it may not have been Basinger's goal. His goal may have simply been a self-serving one – to bring about the first capital case in Putnam County since the nineteenth century. Such a coup would serve his election campaign well.

Any chance Kenny had for bail died when the court granted the prosecution's request to set bail at half a million dollars –

the same as my own bail. The prosecution apparently believed that, if one brother couldn't afford such a sum, neither could the other. It wasn't the only comparison made between us. Basinger also informed the grand jury of my confinement in Washington for murder, making the obvious implication that, if one brother is a murderer, the other must be too.

7

BLOOD BROTHERS

When I shot two people, killing one, I also shot my older brother. He was the unseen victim for my actions would be used to strengthen the case Basinger began to build against Kenny. Basinger used me as a tool to prejudice Kenny's case.

Following Kenny's arrest and confinement in the Putnam County Jail, we began to write regularly. For me, it became a way to try to explain my actions to Kenny as well as to myself, without in any way justifying them. For Kenny, I became an avenue for him to vent his frustrations at the prosecutor and the web in which he found himself entangled. However, other people also read our letters.

Under the instructions of Basinger, all of Kenny's outgoing mail was read and photocopied. Kenny knew this but he continued to make threats against Basinger. 'It was stupid and immature of me,' Kenny reflects. 'But, at the time, I felt it was the only way I could retaliate against the man and relieve some of my anger. The man was playing a game with my life.' Kenny didn't believe his case would see the inside of a courtroom. As soon as the forensic results came back, he optimistically believed he would be released. He believed Basinger had filed the trumped up charges against him for one purpose only – to get himself some fairly sensational publicity to boost his election bid. At most, Kenny believed he'd be tried for the minor breaking and entering charge.

With this mentality, Kenny also wrote letters to friends in Edinburgh and created a fantasy in which he was associated with a heavy gang there. To further scare Basinger, he wrote of having got them to put a hit out on Basinger. He also voiced his threats against Basinger in jail. A jailer overheard him and he would relay the threats to a packed courtroom – thereby becoming another witness to wreck Kenny's character.

If his intention was to scare Basinger, it was a stupid plan that only increased Basinger's determination to put Kenny away. Basinger feared Kenny. Dad told me that, while he voluntarily worked in the Ottawa graveyard pulling weeds one Sunday afternoon, Sergeant Stechschulte saw him as he drove by. He stopped to talk. He informed Dad of the test results from Kenny's clothing and, before Stechschulte drove off, Dad said, 'Basinger is scared of Kenny, isn't he?'

Stechschulte said, 'Yes – but it's no secret he's got a yellow streak in him.'

Realising a scared man with power can be dangerous, Dad warned Kenny to knock it off with the threats. Problem was, it was too late.

On July the fourteenth, four days after Kenny's arson and murder indictment, the court-appointed Attorney William Kluge and Attorney Gregory Donahue to represent him (two lawyers are permitted to be appointed to represent a defendant facing a capital murder case). Attorney Donahue was no more than Kluge's assistant and neither of them had defended an accused in a capital murder trial before.

Although Kenny shouldn't have expected much help from a lawyer, he did. Like the police, the legal profession in a small town is in a class below its counterpart in a big city. Towns like Ottawa are catch-basins for the underachieving – but still ambitious – lawyers who are unable to compete in the cities.

Upon entering a catch-basin like Ottawa and opening an office, a lawyer, just on the strength of his title, receives free memberships to clubs, gets offered a position on the town council and is in line for all sorts of similar perks.

Unable to survive on criminal cases alone, an Ottawa lawyer becomes a jack-of-all-trades. He rarely specialises in one area of law and, instead, he earns the majority of his income from the surrounding farmers by handling mostly administrative law – land claims and titles, insurance claims, wills, bankruptcies, civil suits, that kind of thing. Occasionally a divorce comes along or the odd criminal case, which usually consists of nothing more serious than a drinking and driving charge or an assault. But, for the ambitious lawyer, towns like Ottawa can become the springboard for entry into politics or to becoming a judge. When State elections come around every two years, even if a more competent non-lawyer person runs against a lawyer, more often than not, it is the lawyer who, on the basis of his legal status, is nominated.

Prior to Kenny's arraignment hearing on July the fourteenth, his court-appointed attorneys advised him to plead 'not guilty' to all charges and 'not guilty by reason of insanity' to all charges. Kenny's jaw fell open. He argued bitterly that making the latter plea would make him appear guilty. It was a good point and he was probably right. Kluge, a tall man with a head of curls and an unruly beard, assured Kenny that it wouldn't make him look guilty because he would also plead not guilty. The insanity plea, Kluge advised, was merely a formality so the court would allow a psychological evaluation to be conducted on Kenny – the results of which could provide the defence with mitigating factors to help prevent the imposition of the death sentence should he be found guilty. Kenny didn't believe his case would even see the courtroom so, although unconvinced with this so-called formality, he followed his lawyers' advice. He was, after all, completely ignorant in legal matters.

Being advised to enter such a plea sparked Kenny's first suspicion that his lawyers were ineffective – a suspicion that was to be reinforced over the following months. He would soon be suffering from drowning-man syndrome – where a drowning man grabs at anything in the hope of being able to stay afloat – and, to him, his lawyers' pieces of advice were like life-saving logs bobbing in the water.

On July the seventeenth, Fire Marshal Cryer returned to Hope's burned apartment to take pictures of the fire scene and, for the first time, take away some samples to test. He chipped pieces of concrete from a discoloured heat-cracked area on the living-room floor. He took some woodchips from what he said was a charred area on the balcony deck in front of the sliding glass door at the north inner edge of the deck. And he took more woodchips from a discoloured area four inches from the south outer edge of the balcony deck.

On July the twenty-first, three weeks after the carpet had been retrieved from the county dump, a couple of deputies unrolled it across the asphalt immediately in front of two petrol pumps. The fire marshal cut samples from it. Not long after, the samples, along with Kenny's boots and clothing, were tested.

The wait for the test results brought a period of impatience for Kenny. 'I wish those bloody test results would hurry back,' he wrote to me. 'They'll have to drop the charges then because the results will be negative.' But mostly he wrote of other things and we rarely mentioned the circumstances that had brought us to the point where both of us were facing the possibility of State execution. We optimistically wrote about what we would do when we were released – as if the gates were going to open the next day. For me, it was a form of denial to insulate me from the reality of my situation. I believe I needed this illusion of hope to prevent me from committing suicide.

Kenny, however, truly believed his release was imminent –

he just had to wait until 'after that bastard gets elected'. He wrote of returning to Edinburgh. We both did. We missed home and wrote longingly of it. We shared memories of better times. Confinement does that to you. It throws you into the world of your past. I suppose it's an experience similar to that shared by a person grieving over the death of a loved one. During the grieving process, a person recalls moments spent with the loved one. Confined indefinitely, I grieved for the death of my liberty, reliving memories of good times, trying to forget the pain I inflicted which led to the end of my freedom.

During our time of confinement, Kenny and I communicated on an equal level for the first time ever. Before, as older brothers tend to do, he had had a habit of talking down to me. And brothers often bicker and squabble and we were no different. Our younger brother, Steven, and I got along well and Steven and Kenny got along well but leave Kenny and me in a room for long and we'd be at each other's throats. Yet, in the event of outside threats, we banded together – our blood remained thick. Occasionally, I took advantage of this.

I remembered a time, several weeks after I had changed primary schools from Sighthill to Clermiston because the family had moved from our Sighthill council flat to a posh house in Barnton. I'd been on the receiving end of a difficult time from Podge, the school bully. Podge was three of four years older than me – around the same age as Kenny – and he was too old and too big for me to fight him on my own. Kenny wasn't aware of the problems I had with Podge but, one day, he was waiting outside my school gate. He had probably skipped afternoon classes at his secondary school and had nothing better to do. I met him at the gate and we waited for Steven. Other kids were hanging around the gate too, just talking and messing about. And, as usual, Podge was loitering around with his clan of arse-kissers. He stood tallest among them and brawniest. A man-child, Podge was even much bigger than Kenny but Kenny had a good reputation as a scrapper and I'd yet to see him lose. I believed he could beat anyone.

I elbowed Kenny in the ribs. 'Ye see that laddie there?' I asked him, nodding at Podge. 'He said you and me are wankers.'

With that, Kenny's jaw snapped shut and he stomped towards Podge. A couple of minutes later, Podge lifted himself to his feet, nursing a swollen lip and eye. He never bothered me again.

The closer I got to puberty, the farther apart Kenny and I grew. At the age of sixteen, he left his school in Wester Hailes and found work on a Youth Training Scheme as a waiter in the Barnton Hotel. At four years younger than Kenny, I had just entered that stage of adolescence where football, music, parties and feeling up girls were the things that really mattered. By then, the only times Kenny and I interacted, it seemed, were when he caught me snooping in his room, which would result in me being roughed up a bit.

At around this time, our family's seams started fraying. My dad's business, Amscot Mini-Bus and Coach Charter Company, was hit by financial losses. Sabotage, probably from competition, aggravated the situation. Sugar was poured in vehicle petrol tanks and parts and tools were stolen during a break-in at the company garage. The final blow was a gas heater tank explosion in the company office during the night. The business nosedived. It affected the home. Mum and Dad quarrelled over the smallest thing and their marriage began crumbling, with Kenny, Steven and I being the glue that was only just keeping them together. Soon, even we wouldn't be enough.

Before the end of 1980, my family moved from our Barnton home to my grandad's house in Tollcross, near the heart of Edinburgh. We moved because as Mum put it, 'Grandad can't take care of the house by himself'. This was only partly true – the Barnton house mortgage payments had become a burden. Money wasn't coming in and what little my dad did make he put right back into his business. He was almost a stranger during this period of our lives, working himself to near mental and physical exhaustion. It was a lost cause. His business was barely breathing.

The quarrelling between my parents continued. Kenny and I didn't help matters. He'd begun a pattern of bringing the police to the door and I began skipping school. In fact, I'd missed school so often that my parents and I soon sat before a children's panel. I received a warning. Not only were my parents having difficulty controlling their own lives, they were unable to pull the reins in on Kenny and me. It was a time of chaos in the home and I tried to stay away as much as possible. Kenny moved out and found his own digs.

A few months after Kenny left, Dad also packed and left. He returned to the United States. His nineteen-year marriage was over. He left no explanation for his sudden departure other than a short letter I found beside my bed when I awoke the morning he left. He said he needed time to think and, though he made no mention of returning to America, I somehow knew that was where he'd gone. A more detailed letter for Mum confirmed my suspicions.

Although Dad had left money behind, it wasn't enough and Mum supported Steven and me by pulling pints at the Westfield Bar and Lounge. Within a couple of months, Dad asked us to pack and immigrate to America to start anew but Mum was having none of it. Any chance they had to patch things up ended when Dad had 'abandoned us', as Mum put it. Besides, she disliked living in America, having lived there early in her marriage.

She first met Dad while, as an intelligence officer in the US Air Force, he was stationed at a base outside Edinburgh. They exchanged vows one year later and soon moved to Holland when Dad was assigned to a base in Zeist. They lived in Zeist for eighteen months, during which time Kenny was born on

August the third 1964. Although homesick, Mum followed my dad to America when he left the Air Force. After living for two years in Alabama, amid America's race riots of the period, Mum decided she'd had enough and she returned home to Scotland with Kenny clutching her hand. Soon after, Dad followed and he stayed until he left in July 1982.

Despite Dad's pleas to her to emigrate, Mum refused. Dad then worked on Kenny, Steven and me. Unwilling to leave Mum, Steven and I remained in Edinburgh but Kenny decided he would go. He was on the dole and maybe Reagan's America could offer something Thatcher's Britain couldn't. He wishes he had stayed home.

When Kenny left for America, the distance in our relationship grew. It wasn't until our time in jail, two thousand miles apart, that Kenny and I became closer than we had ever been. Regardless of our differences, we came to realise one thing hadn't changed. Pressured by outside threats, we banded together – our blood remained thick.

I cared little about his guilt or innocence – he was my brother and that is all that mattered. Besides, who was I to judge, given my own actions? Yet, I did believe his claims of innocence because I just couldn't imagine him killing a child. This was the thing that really disturbed me about his situation. Kenny adored children and I couldn't believe he was capable of starting a fire, knowing it could jeopardise a child's life. So, yes, I believed he was innocent. I believed the fire was not caused by arson and I believed the charges against him were an election tactic by Basinger. I believed these things until the lab reports were returned on the evidence samples. Despite Kenny's claims of innocence, I found it difficult to dispute incriminating evidence.

The concrete chips taken from the discoloured area of the living-room floor tested negative for the presence of accelerants. The woodchips taken from the north inner edge of the balcony, the charred area, also tested negative and the boots and clothing

Kenny had worn on the night of the fire also tested negative. However, three samples tested positive. One woodchip taken four inches from the south outer edge of the balcony, an unburned area, tested positive for the presence of paint thinner. One sample cut from the carpet also tested positive for paint thinner and another sample of the carpet tested positive for a trace of petrol.

I learned about the lab reports two and a half weeks after Kenny and the rest of Putnam County did. I had been receiving a letter once a week from Kenny and, in each, he complained about the delay of the test results. Then, no letter. When I again received no letter the following week, I knew the lab reports had come back and I knew they were unfavourable.

When Kenny finally did write, he was a changed man. He sounded desperate. He wrote of a set-up, claiming that the authorities had tampered with the evidence in order to make the charges against him stick. He threatened Basinger more. He threatened the fire marshal. 'Dishonest bastards,' he called them.

I wanted to believe in his innocence but now doubts started creeping into my mind. I still believed he couldn't have started the fire *knowing* a child slept in the flat but I had to believe that the fire had been caused by arson. After all, they had found the presence of flammable liquids. I couldn't believe Kenny's accusation that the authorities intentionally contaminated the evidence. But maybe my trust in the system was naive.

Others, not knowing Kenny as well as I did, could only determine his guilt or innocence by rumour and the facts – the positive test results. All that the people of Putnam County knew about Kenny was that he had a criminal record, he was a foreigner and he had wasted away his days with the aimless crowd at the Old Farm Village Apartment Complex. They knew that he'd been arrested for arson and murder resulting from an alleged threat he made and that traces of accelerants had been discovered in the burnt apartment. Adding gossip to the fact that his brother sat in jail for murder in Washington State, the general consensus was summed up by one woman. She wrote a letter, printed in the editor's section of the county newspaper. She scathingly stated that they should forget about wasting their good taxpaying dollars on a trial. Kenny Richey is guilty and everyone knows it – they should strap the child-killer to an electric chair now.

When a football team scores a goal, it's never accomplished by one player walking up the field, unchallenged, and then kicking the ball to the back of the net. The goal is achieved by passes and dribbles. As with the community prejudice against Kenny, this prejudice couldn't solely convict him. It was simply a pass or a dribble.

About a month after the lab reports had kicked Kenny in the belly, he wrote of other developments about his case. His lawyers advised him to waive his right to a trial by jury because they believed they would be unable to find twelve unbiased jury members from the community. Instead of a jury trial, his lawyers recommended he assert his right to a bench trial. A bench trial, which consists of a panel of three presiding judges, would provide him with, his lawyers assured, untainted viewpoints. Naturally, Kenny heeded their advice. It was a mistake. The odds for success are greater with a jury – the defence need only convince one person out of twelve jurors that the case the prosecution has presented is flawed. In a bench trial, the defence had the considerably tougher job of convincing one out of three.

If Kenny's lawyers were concerned about jury bias, they should have requested a change of venue. This common practice would have allowed Kenny to be tried hundreds of miles away in another part of the State. These procedural errors, which Kenny was unaware of at the time, screamed of incompetence. Cash poor defendants have enough to contend with without an incompetent defence. But, unfortunately, defence incompetence is all too often a handicap that some must overcome. In America, only the wealthy can be guaranteed competent legal representation.

Shortly after the lab results were returned, Merrian C. Blye, the former co-manager of the apartment complex, paid a visit to Dad. She informed him that, on several occasions, she reprimanded Hope's husband for cleaning car parts in the apartment with petrol. Also, she told him that she had supplied Hope with paint thinner on two occasions after instructing her to fill and paint a hole that had been kicked through her living-room wall. Hope had told Mrs Blye that she needed the paint thinner to clean a paint spill in the living room that had happened when she had been fixing the hole.

Dad believed the information could be useful. Mrs Blye would make a credible witness – she had been a prison officer and had also worked for the police. Dad contacted Kluge and relayed the information Mrs Blye had supplied. But then Dad slipped back into his fog. Understandably, the predicaments Kenny and I were in affected our parents. In Dad's words, 'After losing Tom and then Kenny, I closed myself in my apartment, wrapped myself in a cocoon and tried to forget what was going on. When I emerged, I went through the motions of living. I went through those months in a fog, trying to pretend that it just didn't happen. I nearly lost my sanity. If it was not for Steven (who travelled to America in August 1986), I couldn't begin to guess the outcome.'

Kluge promised Dad he would interview Merrian Blye but he never did. It was yet another example of bad lawyering. Another witness was also strangely absent from the defence witness list – the Columbus Grove Fire Chief, Len Hefner. Following his investigation of the apartment, he declared that the fire's cause was electrical. He never wavered from this opinion yet, incredibly, Kluge wouldn't call him to the stand to oppose Fire Marshal Cryer.

As the days entered the month of November, the election buzz hit the State and every city and town within its boundaries. When the ballots were tallied, Assistant Prosecutor Basinger had a new title – Judge Basinger. However, because he had built the case against Kenny, he decided to finish prosecuting it and don his black robe after it was over. Not only would it be the most significant case he'd ever prosecute, it would be his last.

Then an unusual thing happened. Judge Basinger offered Kenny a deal – a plea bargain. Basinger proposed that, if Kenny pled guilty to a lesser murder charge, he would receive a sentence of eleven years. That would allow him the chance for parole after he served six years. Kenny took a stance. He'd made the decision that he would never plead guilty again for something he didn't do and he stood by that decision. He flatly refused the plea bargain.

It was an exceptional plea bargain, to be sure. For example, I faced an aggravated murder charge at the time too and the plea-bargain offer extended to me was a term of sixty-five years in exchange for a plea of guilt as an alternative to facing the death penalty. If Basinger truly believed Kenny was guilty of murder, he never would have offered such a bargain. To offer a man you claim to be a psychotic child killer the chance for release after six years is akin to a slap on the wrist, particularly in a country known for its excessive sentencing practices. And what supports Kenny's claim that Basinger built the case based on political motivation is that he only offered the plea bargain after the elections – after the case served his purpose.

Kenny's preliminary trial was set for December the twelfth. The preliminary trial, less formal than the trial, handles multiple issues such as determining whether legal procedures were adhered to during the seizure of evidence. It's a setting to address anything remotely connected with a defendant's case.

Early in the morning of December the twelfth, following a

jailhouse breakfast, two deputies stepped in front of Kenny's cell. They strip-searched him according to procedure. 'Arms in the air. Let me see your hands, front and back. Armpits. Behind the ears. Mouth, open wide – lift you tongue. Hair – run your hands through vigorously. Penis – lift it up. Scrotum sack – lift it up. Good. Now turn around. Let me see the bottoms of your feet. Wiggle your toes. That's good. Now bend over and spread your ass cheeks. OK, get dressed.'

Kenny got dressed into the underwear and orange overalls that had been searched by one deputy while the other deputy conducted the degrading body search. Civilian clothes were unnecessary – even the lawyers wouldn't wear jackets or ties at the preliminary trial. When Kenny stepped from the cell, he was handcuffed and then escorted from the jail to the county courthouse, a short distance along the street. Flanked by the deputies and blinded by a clear chilly sun, Kenny remembers it as the closest to freedom he'd been in months. It was all so surreal. Only months before, he'd been driving through these streets. Now he was the most despised man in Putnam County and he was fighting for his life. No one would listen to his claims of innocence. He couldn't explain why the three samples had tested positive for accelerants. Of course, he didn't know about the information provided by Merrian Blye – Dad had told Kluge but he'd neglected to tell Kenny. Dad was tormented seeing Kenny in jail and he only visited a few times and, then, only for short periods. They spoke little about his case, both wishing to avoid the subject as if, by not mentioning his situation, it would just disappear. Besides, Dad had no reason to suspect that Kluge wouldn't run with the information. As far as he knew, Kluge had told Kenny.

The courthouse is a great sandblasted stone building that stands in an island of well-trimmed grass, looking prominent amid the surrounding wooden homes. Kenny found it intimidating. With its imposing arches, Roman pillars and great oak doors, power emanated from the structure. His fate would be determined behind those doors.

When they entered the surprisingly packed courtroom, the deputies led him to the defence table. The crowded room surprised Kenny because he knew the informal proceedings would hardly be entertaining. Of course, he realised that they hadn't come to view the proceedings as much as they'd come to see the monster who'd come into their midst. The deputies removed his handcuffs and he sat next to his lawyers who greeted him with silent nods. One of the deputies stood against the white-washed wall to the left of the defence table and the second deputy positioned himself by the door. Kenny turned in his chair and faced our dad and Steven. Tentative smiles cracked their anxious faces.

When the county prosecutor, Daniel Gershultz, and Basinger entered the courtroom moments after Kenny, Steven could almost see the daggers shooting from Kenny's eyes. Dad had to nudge him and tell him to settle down.

Basinger acted unconcerned, but he refused to meet Kenny's eyes. If he had, my dad believed it would have triggered Kenny to spring from his chair. Kenny remained tense. When the bailiff called, 'All rise for the Honorable Judge Corrigan presiding.' Kenny stood up stiffly.

The ensuing proceedings touched on many issues. To Kenny's relief, Kluge withdrew the plea of 'not guilty by reason of insanity' though the damage of this plea had already been done. He also waived Kenny's right to a trial by jury. Motions previously filed were addressed. These included the motion to suppress Kenny's recorded statements and the motion to quash the breaking and entering charge – without Kenny's confession that he had broken into the greenhouse, no evidence existed of the break-in because no fingerprints had been taken and no signs of forced entry were evident. However, both motions were denied.

Strangely, Kenny's lawyers failed to attack the more serious charges – the procedural issues regarding the Waiver of Rights form that Kenny claimed was a forgery and the lack of his consent for the interview statements to be taped. Kluge did file a motion to suppress the latter but, when the court denied the motion, he failed to pursue the issue further.

The prosecutor's side introduced new evidence – three letters they had seized. Two of the letters had been written by Kenny to his friends in Edinburgh and both of them contained threats against Basinger. The third letter had been obtained, by means of a search warrant, from our dad's apartment. The letter had been written by me to Dad. It contained an admission of guilt for my crimes. After introducing the letters, the prosecution called six witnesses. The questions posed pertained to arrest and evidence procedures. Dad was also called to the witness stand and questioned about the letter that had been seized by Sergeant Stechschulte.

Asked why my letter was taken as evidence, Sergeant Stechschulte said, 'To try to form a basis for some type of violent action to see if there was any . . . I don't know how to phrase it . . . any coalition or conjunction with his brother, Tom.'

In other words, Stechschulte was looking for something to support the contention that Kenny and I were evil brothers. In presenting the letter as evidence to the court, it was also Basinger's strategy to remind the court that I had committed murder in Washington and, if one brother is a murderer . . .

The proceedings ended with a date being set for the commencement of trial – January the fifth 1987, less than one month away.

8

BLEAK MIDWINTER

Kenny returned to his cell, numbed by the proceedings. The seriousness on the faces of the witnesses as they took the stand and were sworn in served to remind him that his situation was no longer the game he thought Basinger was playing. He'd refused the plea bargain and Basinger intended to put him to death by State execution. Yet, despite all that, it seemed unbelievable and it was an outcome he just couldn't grasp. As he explained, 'I was innocent and, no matter what evidence they brought to the courtroom, I was confident the judges would find me not guilty. That belief was like a light at the end of the tunnel. I just didn't realise the light was actually coming from a freight train heading in my direction.'

He only had to stand the conditions of jail for a wee while longer, he told himself. He'd lived in the tiny airless cell for nearly six months and the time had dragged. He'd spent much of his days writing letters, using the daylight that struggled through the bars of the tiny safety-glass window. He had only been allowed out of the cell for two hours a day, weather permitting, to breathe fresh air in a chain-link fenced yard, its area no larger than a basketball court. A basketball was allowed but he usually used it to kick at an imaginary goal against the fence until the guard ordered him to stop. For the other twenty-two hours, he had his thoughts and letters to while away his time. But there's only so many letters a person can write and his conversations between cells with the jail's temporary inmates turned stale (inmates could only communicate through the bars of their cells).

A cardboard box brimming with books sat at the end of the landing. Initially, Kenny didn't venture into the box. If a book contained no pictures, it didn't interest him. But, before long, boredom carried him to the book box and he sauntered back, carrying something thin. Within the first few pages, he hunted KGB agents on the streets of London. And so began his love of books. He voraciously read any novel set in Britain and, although he hated how the stories aggravated his longing to return home, he loved how they allowed him to be there.

As January the fifth neared, his lawyers advised that he abstain from taking the stand. Although most defendants don't take the stand, Kenny believed it would make him appear as if he was trying to hide something. However, his lawyers feared Basinger would attack him. His line of questioning was bound to lead to Kenny having to reveal the threats he'd made against Basinger and the fire marshal in his letters. His lawyers also feared that Basinger would make Kenny reveal his attempted suicide, his commitment to a mental institution and his previous criminal record. They also feared that Basinger would trigger an angry outburst from Kenny. He didn't have to testify anyway, they told him, because he had accounted for his movements during the taped interrogation that the panel of judges deciding the trial would hear. He heeded their advice and agreed that he wouldn't take the stand.

Christmas passed like any other day in jail for Kenny. His jailers served slightly larger portions of food but nothing else separated the day from any other. Still it didn't feel like any other day no matter how much he tried to treat it as such. Steven and our dad had visited him the day before, bringing him cigarettes and magazines so at least he had something to read and cigarettes to smoke.

As nineteen-eighty-seven established itself, Kenny began to notice that his hands often trembled. He smoked heavily, leading to unsightly nicotine stains on his fingers. On January the fourth, he erased the stains with the rough side of a matchbox. He also sat in a makeshift barber's chair that day. The barber was a prisoner serving a couple of weeks for drunk driving and, not trusting the man's hairdressing skills, Kenny opted for a crew cut – few can mess up a crew cut.

After breakfast on the morning of the fifth, he shaved. The jailer brought his personal clothing, and he strip-searched Kenny before allowing him to dress. He didn't own a suit but Dad had offered to bring one of his. However, even in the worst of times, vanity plays its hand. Kenny refused to wear our dad's 'older style' and, instead, wore brogues, charcoal pleated trousers and a white shirt.

When the jailer opened his cell door, he asked Kenny if he was ready. He nodded and then half-smiled. 'Aye,' he said, 'as ready as I'll ever be, I suppose.'

His trial was to last three days.

9

THE TRIAL

Not even standing room remained in the courtroom.

At 8.28 a.m., gowned in black robes, three judges came through the door leading from their chambers and stepped up to the bench. They sat side by side. The 'three monkeys', Kenny later christened them, explaining that they 'see no truth, hear no truth, speak no truth'. Officially known as Michael J. Corrigan, Donald Nugent and Charles Abood, these three monkeys in their Darth Vader robes would decide Kenny's fate. At eight-thirty, the trial commenced.

Although Dad was prohibited from entering the courtroom until called as a witness, Kenny did have the support of our blonde-haired brother who sat in the front row behind Kenny. Clearly, Steven was his only support. Out of the silence that followed when Kenny shuffled into the courtroom in leg chains and handcuffs, somebody hissed, 'Baby killer!'

Kenny's head snapped toward the sea of faces, searching. It could have been any one of them. They all sneered. One woman had even pinned an enlarged photo of Cynthia to her chest, wearing it all through the trial. As Kenny said of his courtroom entrance, 'I'm innocent but, when I saw the rotten looks from all those people, it was enough to make me feel guilty of something.'

Judge Corrigan, the leading judge, spoke. 'Let the record

reflect we are here this morning in the case of the State versus Richey, case number CR eighty-six dash twenty-one. First of all, there are some preliminary matters the court wants to take care of. There was a request in the jury room by the State that the defendant be shackled during the course of the proceedings . . .' And so the judges decided that, though Kenny's hands would be unrestrained, his legs would stay chained together through-out the trial – shackled, as if already found guilty.

After the December the twelfth preliminary trial, Kenny's lawyers had filed a motion to suppress the three letters seized by the sheriff's department. The three judges granted the motion to throw out the letters but the ruling made no difference. Basinger had already achieved his purpose by introducing the letters. The three judges had read them and again my offence was impressed on their minds, as were Kenny's threats against Basinger. Presumably, this was behind their decision to keep Kenny shackled during the trial. And, although the letters were rejected as evidence, the judges couldn't obliterate from their minds what they had already read.

Moments later, to the vocal dissatisfaction of the spectators, the judges discussed viewing the scene of the alleged crime – the empty apartment Hope Collins once lived in. Basinger had made the necessary arrangements and police cruisers lined the kerb outside. The judges, the stenographer, the prosecution and the defence left the courtroom and drove to the Old Farm Village Apartment Complex. As the others went to look at the scene of the fire, Kenny sat in the rear of one of the cruisers, unable to get out. One of the kids he used to take camping stood near the pavement, staring curiously at the vehicles. Kenny smiled and waved at the boy. When the boy responded by turning his back on Kenny and running away, he realised that, no matter what the outcome of the trial might be, he would never be able to return to the complex again.

After viewing Hope's apartment and the greenhouse, as well

as the position of our dad's apartment in relation to Hope's, everyone returned to the courtroom. Further preliminary matters were attended to. The rule existed that no witness could enter the courtroom before being called to testify for the obvious reason that, if a witness wished to take sides, they need only corroborate another witness's testimony. Kluge requested that the court applied that rule to Sergeant Stechschulte who sat behind the prosecution's table with Basinger and Gershultz and was due to be called as a witness for the State. The panel of judges denied the request for his removal, reasoning that, since Stechschulte was the investigating officer of the case, he could remain in the courtroom to assist the prosecutors in the presentation of their case.

Kluge then asked the court to caution Stechschulte and all other witnesses against discussing, consulting or advising uncalled witnesses of testimony or evidence already presented to the court. But, once more, the panel denied the request. Judge Corrigan stated, 'I'm not going to do that. If they choose to speak with other individuals, you're certainly welcome to inquire about that and test their credibility but I'm not going to enforce a gag rule upon the witnesses.'

Seconds later, the panel called Basinger to begin opening statements, a monologue of several thousand words stacked with incredible allegations that the ensuing trial proved were complete drivel.

'It took all my strength to stop myself from jumping up and throttling that bastard then and there,' Kenny said, regarding Basinger's opening statement. But he just sat there, his face becoming redder and redder the longer Basinger spoke.

In essence, Basinger portrayed Kenny as a psychotic killer. Basinger said that, from the day of Candy Barchet's arrival at the apartment complex, Kenny had struck up an 'obsessive, compulsive sexual/romantic relationship'. He claimed that, until two days before the fire, Kenny was obsessed with Candy, that he was 'hedonistic and sociopathic' in his relationship with Candy Barchet.

'No one else could be around her,' Basinger continued, as he paced the courtroom floor. 'During that period of time, he [Kenny] repeatedly said to others, "If I can't have her, no one else will." And he told Candy, "If I can't have you, then no one else will. I'll kill anyone else you're with."' He then described how, a week before the fire, their relationship got stormier. An incident had occurred on June the twenty-fourth in which the defendant, supposedly still Candy Barchet's lover at the time, had found Candy in bed with John Butler. He had pulled a knife, made threats, put on his marine camouflage outfit, which he would want to do in this sort of situation, and made threats about killing anyone she was with.

During the week leading up to the fire, the relationship had continued to be a stormy one. The threats had continued – in fact, the threats had increased. Candy Barchet had become frightened of the defendant and his violent possessive statements. His attitude towards her and anyone else that she was ever seen talking to had scared her and the threatening statements had become more and more frequent. This had continued up to the weekend before the fire. On Saturday and Sunday, Candy had been with a new lover – Mike Nichols. The defendant had then begun to plan to make good on his threats to kill anyone else she was with – that, if he couldn't have her, no one else will.

If Kenny had made threats to kill anyone Candy was with and if he was a hedonistic sociopath, wouldn't such a person have reacted violently in the incident with John Butler? Kenny had even had a weapon. As Basinger put it, 'He pulled a knife.' Had Kenny, in his deranged obsessive state, plunged the knife into John Butler's chest? No. He had thrown the knife on the floor and said, 'I don't want to hurt you.'

'In the week preceding the fire,' Basinger went on, 'the

relationship continued on a stormy basis. The threats continued – the threats increased. Candy Barchet became frightened . . .'

Was he talking about another case? As Kluge would ask Candy during cross-examination, 'Regarding your relationship with Kenny, let's go back to the time you told him the relationship was over. It was the Wednesday or Thursday before June thirtieth, is that correct?' (This would make it the day after the John Butler incident.)

'That's correct,' Candy answered.

'At that time, how did Kenny take it?'

'He really didn't say too much about it.'

'OK, did he voice any objection to not seeing you any more?'

'No, he did not.'

'Did he ever get angry at you because of that?'

'No.'

'Like he wanted you, he couldn't live without you – "I'll love you forever." – things like that?'

'No.'

'From the time you started seeing Mike Nichols, did Kenny express any of those things I just asked you about? That he couldn't live without you or that he wanted you?'

'No, he did not.'

Clearly, as the trial progressed, Basinger assassinated Kenny's character almost every time he breathed. Of course, it was his job and I'm sure it is part of every prosecutor's strategy but Basinger leaned on this so heavily one has to wonder if it is because the material evidence was so weak?

As Basinger continued with his opening statement, he described the party, the heavy drinking, the incident between Kenny and Mike, Kenny's alleged threats to burn or bomb A-building, his alleged volunteering to babysit Cynthia and his alleged burning of the apartment after pouring a combination of accelerants over the living room and balcony.

As expected, Basinger made no mention of Kenny's attempt

to enter the burning apartment – that would make Kenny look too human. All Basinger said was that Kenny stood on the breezeway, yelling, 'The baby's in there, the baby's in there! Get the baby out!' Then he described how the firemen came on the scene, wearing masks and tanks. 'The defendant during this whole period was still out on the [breezeway] landing, making new threats to policemen and firemen and anyone else who was around about "wiping you out" and whatever he chose to make threats about.'

Basinger paused before the panel of judges. 'The apartment fire is put out, the smoke is still heavy, the furniture is still smouldering. The firemen at the scene are numerous – thirty or forty probably altogether, including firemen (sic), policemen, all the other people milling around the scene. Candy Barchet asks the firemen if she can go back into her apartment to get some diapers for her small child. The fireman says, "Alright." We're talking minutes after the fire. She goes into the apartment and the defendant follows her in. He says, "What are you doing in here?" And she says, "Getting diapers for my child." He says, "There's a fire here and all you care about is diapers for your child?" She says, "Yeah, I need diapers for my child." He kneels beside her and says, "Did the fire scare you?" and she says, "Yes, the fire scared me." And the defendant says, "I told you, if I couldn't have you, no one else would."

'He then walks over, picks up a beer off the counter, pops a beer. The fire is essentially in progress, pops a beer (sic), then walks out below Hope Collins' apartment. As a smouldering chair is being thrown out of the apartment, the defendant looks up and Juanita Altimus hears him say, "I guess I did a good job, didn't I?" and then he laughs.

'A short time later, Candy Barchet and Mike Nichols are on the other side of the apartment. The defendant walks over and he says to the two of them, as they're standing there, "If your boyfriend thinks he's so bad, why don't we settle this right now?" We're talking within minutes of the fire. The fire department is still out there, putting the fire out. This man,' Basinger said, pointing at Kenny across the courtroom, 'macho, is still confronting people, is still making threats to people . . .'

Yet, Police Chief Miller and two other deputies would testify that, immediately after removing Kenny from the breezeway landing, they placed him in the rear of the police cruiser. Unable to get out, he remained inside the cruiser until the chief took him to the police station. Two other officers confirmed this, as did Kenny's signed and dated statement that Miller took at the station. Kenny couldn't have been two places at once. Mike Nichols, Candy Barchet and Juanita Altimus, as it turned out, were to be no more credible than many of the other witnesses who were paraded in that courtroom.

After using the first few thousand words of his opening statement to deliberately portray Kenny as a lunatic, Basinger made the transition to speaking about the fire itself. He said, 'The evidence will show that, when the fire was being put out, several people were in danger. The ceiling fell in on the firemen. The fire essentially gutted the entire living-room area of the Collins' apartment. And, certainly, everyone at the complex was at risk. After the fire was put out, the State fire marshal's office conducted an extensive investigation. Their investigation, the evidence will show beyond all doubt that it was an arson. There is simply no question. Six separate points confirmed that fact.

'The first and foremost – the intensity of the flame. The flames within a forty-minute period were in the carpet area and the balcony area, where there was nothing to burn – essentially a ball of flame from top to bottom – and the photos that the State of Ohio is going to present, along with the testimony, is going to leave no other conclusion.'

Holding up a couple of fingers, Basinger said, 'Two – the carpet in that living room was essentially burned all the way through, right down to the concrete. Half of the room's carpet was burned where there was simply nothing left. The time element as to how long the fire took place? The fire was a maximum of forty minutes. The State fire marshal is going to say there is simply no way a fire without the use of accelerants could have progressed that severely – that quickly – that intensely – unless there had been accelerants used to create the ball of flame and that fire in that apartment.

'Three – the charring on the balcony and in the other locations. The balcony itself was burned and the timbers on that balcony were charred through. The fire from inside the apartment simply did not do that. The balcony was burned like that because there were accelerants on the balcony itself, placed there by the defendant. And you will see pictures where the accelerants seeped through the cracks of the balcony and burned the timbers, burned the grooves, burned on separate igniting areas, which the fire marshal's office will say conclusively demonstrate the use of accelerants.

'Four – accelerants were found. The carpet was pulled out and taken to a landfill. At my request, later on, it was retrieved and portions of it were sent to the State forensic lab. Along with portions of the carpet, portions of the balcony, which was still intact on the apartment, were also sent. And three areas of the accelerants were placed there by this man.' Again, Basinger jabbed his finger in Kenny's direction.

'Five – all other factors for this fire were eliminated. A fan was considered a problem in that the fan was face down on the floor. Our forensic experts have analysed the fan and say the cut-off switch was intact – did not start the fire. This was not an electrical fire. There was no other source. It was the accelerants.

'Six – the defence's own expert witness confirmed the theory of the fire and confirmed the accelerants. The defence hired an expert witness in this case. I talked with him on the phone. His testimony will be that accelerants were used according to findings and that the theory of the fire marshal's office was correct. The State of Ohio intends to call the defence expert as our own witness.

'An investigation was also conducted by the Putnam County Sheriff's Department. The investigation confirmed the sequence of events that I have discussed, confirmed the repeated statements of this defendant about making threats through and up to the time of the fire and after the fire. The defendant was also questioned after he was arrested. He was questioned by the sheriff's deputy. I believe the evidence will show that he gave several conflicting statements about what happened that night, about his knowledge on several important points.

'He acknowledged he had been drinking heavily. One thing stands out in all the defendant's statements and that is his repeated statement that, "I was so drunk, I don't remember what happened."'

Not once did Kenny make this statement. He did say, 'I was so drunk, I can't really remember.' but he said this in reference to irrelevant matters such as whether or not he saw the fan lying on its face when he visited Hope's bathroom earlier in the evening.

Basinger droned on, 'Well, I think the evidence will show that this is simply not true. He does remember what happened and what happened is he poured a series of accelerants through the apartment and ignited them with total disregard for anyone. The evidence will show that, on the thirtieth of June, this defendant caused the death of Cynthia Collins in committing an aggravated arson. The evidence will show that, when he committed that act, the aggravated arson, he was a principal offender in the commission of that aggravated murder and that offence is punishable by death or imprisonment for life.

'The evidence will show that, on the thirtieth of June 1986, this defendant did knowingly create a substantial risk of serious physical harm to Cynthia Collins. The evidence will show that, on that day, by force, stealth or deception, this defendant trespassed on an unoccupied structure, being McAdam's Commercial Greenhouse, with the purpose being to commit therein a theft offence – something he admits, by the way. The evidence will show that, on that date, he caused the death of Cynthia Collins as a proximate result of committing a felony, being child endangering (*sic*). And the evidence will show that, on that date, the defendant, having custody or control of Cynthia Collins, created a substantial risk to the safety or health of that child, resulting in serious physical harm – that all of these occurred in the village of Columbus Grove, Putnam County.

'The evidence in this case, Your Honours, is going to be overwhelming that, in a hedonistic total disregard for anyone, this defendant committed an aggravated arson back on the thirtieth of June that took the life of Cynthia Collins, took the life of a two-year-old, who was sleeping in the back bedroom, that had nothing to do with this but that, clearly, he didn't care anything about. That during that period, he was attempting to murder Candy Barchet and Mike Nichols but he did, in effect, murder Cynthia Collins.'

Basinger ended his opening statements by making strongly repetitive allegations that were obviously intended to make impressions in the minds of the judges.

Judge Corrigan then called Kluge to begin his opening statements. His statements were, in my opinion, timid – after I had read both, it was Basinger's statements that lingered in my mind.

Kluge got up from behind the defence table and nodded at Basinger as he passed. He faced the judges.

'May it please the court, Your Honours, you have heard what Mr Basinger expects the evidence to be and, to some extent and up to a certain point, we agree with him in part. We agree, for example, with the fact there was a tremendous party going on on the evening of June thirtieth. We agree that practically everyone at the party was either under the influence of drugs, alcohol or both. And we agree, further, that a lot of the people that the State intends to call – and you will see them being paraded in front of you – are nothing more than people who lived to party. Some have no visible means of support. Some do but many have criminal records which show where their incomes come from. We're going to show you a society here that accepts no responsibilities, that lives for the joy of drinking alcohol, that lives for the joy of taking different types of drugs. And I'm not excepting Kenny from that group either.

'I'm going to tell you right now that, on that particular night, Kenny had an awful lot of liquor and beer to consume, that he may or may not have imbibed in the use of drugs, controlled substances, but I want to tell you that many of the State's key witnesses fall into that category that I'm sure you've all seen before – people who do nothing but party all the time, sleep until two in the afternoon, drink all night, stay up till four in the morning. This is the kind of people that the State are going to rely on to convict Kenny Richey.

'Now up to a certain point, and again you will hear varying testimony from the witnesses as to when statements were made about A-building going to burn, what exactly was said and how much they had to consume. All those different things that go into the totality of the circumstances surrounding each statement allegedly made by Mr Richey will indicate to you that there is a basic and inherent unreliability to any statement that may have been made by Mr Richey and/or the way they were interpreted by the witnesses who will testify for the State.

'With that backdrop in mind and without going into the exact nature of what the defence's case will be, I have pinpointed several areas that I feel are key in this case: relating to the physical evidence of the fire; the presence of accelerants in the carpet; to what extent does the carpet having been in the dump affect that?; to what extent other incidents where paint thinner or petrol might have been used to clean up paint spills on the carpet influence the fire marshal's findings?'

Kluge's last sentence is proof that he was aware of the information provided by Merrian Blye through Dad – proof that he knew of Mrs Blye's important information. Why he failed to call Mrs Blye to the witness stand remains a mystery.

Kluge raised his hands before him, saying, 'Where did the accelerants come from? As the State goes through the case, I will ask you to think of where in this forty-minute period those accelerants came from and, if Mr Richey was as drunk as he himself stated and as many witnesses will state, how he could pour paint thinner and gasoline on the carpet without the presence of any accelerants on his clothing?

'There will be no testimony as to the presence of accelerants anywhere on Mr Richey's clothing or anywhere on his belongings. I would ask this court to take note of the fact that the condition of Mr Richey that night was such that not only was he under the influence of alcohol and/or drugs but, at the time, his hand was in a full cast as a result of the incident which happened some days prior would indicate that those two conditions existed at the time of the fire my client is alleged to have started, would indicate whether or not, as the State suggests, that Candy Barchet jilted him is sufficient motive for the defendant to go ahead and start a fire, notwithstanding the fact he knew Cynthia Collins was in the bedroom.

'I don't think there is any question he knew that Cynthia Collins was in that bedroom and I would ask the court to consider carefully his actions, upon arriving at the scene of the fire, would indicate to the court, that from the time the defendant ran from C-building to building A, where the fire was occurring, he was stopped on the landing from entering after he tried to enter (sic). He was forced out by local firemen from the Columbus Grove Fire Department. He was, thereafter, in such an agitated and excited condition, he was restrained by firemen and police officers.

'At approximately 4.30 a.m., the chief of the Columbus Grove Police Department arrived, Tom Miller, and Mr Richey was immediately escorted from the breezeway landing outside Hope Collins' apartment to the police cruiser where he sat until ten after six a.m., wherein he was taken down to the Columbus Grove Police Department to make a short statement and then returned back to the scene at 6.30 a.m. This would categorically and unequivocally make any testimony of any witness, after he appeared back at the landing during the fire, subject to some speculation and we intend to bring that out as all these Columbus Grove firemen and policemen appear before you.'

Kluge never moved from his spot in front of the judges. He stood ramrod straight and he reminded Kenny of a blabbering schoolchild in front of his headmaster. However, he thought Kluge's nearly incoherent ramblings were lawyer talk. 'Finally,' Kluge said, 'there remains the issue of criminal responsibility. And, I guess, one of the big things that has always bothered me about this case is not only is the State alleging that my client deliberately started the fire and caused the death of this poor little girl but they're saying, if you don't believe that, then we're going to ask you to believe he was left as the custodian of that child and, therefore, falls under the child endangering (sic) statute as the custodian and we're going to get him on the child-endangering aspect.

'There are a lot of inconsistencies in the physical evidence that don't jibe with what is going to be testified about. I would ask the court to pay very close attention to the circumstances surrounding what each of these street people or nomads are going to testify about and, in particular, the testimony of Hope Collins. Hope Collins, the mother who was convicted of involuntary manslaughter and child endangering, the mother who gave this poor little two-and-a-half-year-old girl sleeping pills so she wouldn't get up at night, the mother who cares so much about her daughter that she left her with anyone, many times runs off without a babysitter and, in particular, whose credibility is almost zero. Your Honours, thank you very much for listening to me and, again, I ask you to pay very careful attention to all the witnesses. Thank you.'

Like Basinger, Kluge assassinated the character of people involved with the case, particularly Hope Collins. Granted Hope's credibility and responsibility left a lot to be desired but the character attacks, in Kenny's opinion, were in bad taste – manipulations to win by prejudice. Instead, Kenny believed Kluge should have centred his attack on the physical evidence that was meant to support the arson theory. By trial's end, Kluge apparently more or less accepted the arson theory because he barely made any effort to question it. Kluge's performance seemed to express, 'Well, if it was arson, it was not Kenneth Richey who was responsible.'

After a five minute recess following Kluge's opening statements, Judge Corrigan called the first witness.

KEY WITNESSES

The witness testimony that filled the courtroom was confusing, contradictory verbiage. I have spent many hours reading, cross-checking and analysing the testimonies and inevitably there's some uncertainty about the accuracy of instances of *when* something happened, *how* it happened or, indeed, *if* it really happened. It took me some time, through the process of reason, elimination and character validity, to shovel away the dirt and the inconsistencies to reach the most believable conclusions – the facts. Although the three judges were presumably highly intelligent, I will never be convinced they could have seen the truth through that fog of lies – especially when they only had a single opportunity to listen to each of the testimonies.

Had the trial occurred in a city courtroom, the vigilant media would have swooped on it and it would have produced more entertainment than the newspaper's comic section. As one stranger remarked to Dad after leaving the courtroom on the third day, 'In all my years of attending trials, I've never seen a case like this. It's a farce.'

Unfortunately, there were few people like him at the trial. It seemed as if the good people of Putnam County wanted a lynching and a lynching they were going to have. It made little difference if one witness testified to one thing and another testified to something else entirely. The American legal standard of having to find someone guilty beyond reasonable doubt didn't exist in the Putnam County courthouse in this trial.

Even the most important witness, the man Basinger claimed to lead the arson investigation, contradicted others as well as himself. It could be argued that this man, Fire Marshal Robert Cryer, dispensed fabrications as often as a vending machine dispenses Cokes on a hot day. On the stand, he dispensed different answers to questions previously asked. Kenny believed Kluge should have focused on these and other inconsistencies but Kluge rarely did. It would be another vital mistake by the defence.

The subject of impeaching one of the witnesses, Mike Nichols, did arise during trial but Kluge failed to pursue the matter. When there are contradictions between witnesses' accounts and inconsistencies in evidence, it is sometimes the case that a court will acquit the defendant. Given the contradictions and inconsistencies in this case, Basinger should at least have recorded an entry of *nolle prosequi* – 'we will prosecute no further'. However, this was to be the last case Basinger would ever prosecute and few men wish to end their career on a sour note.

HOPE COLLINS

By the time of the trial, Hope was a resident of Lima and, when her divorce became final two months earlier, she had resumed using her maiden name of McName. She entered the courtroom wearing white athletic shoes, tight jeans and a grey peasant blouse. She sat in the witness box with her hands clasped in her lap and her head lowered. She avoided Kenny's eyes.

Basinger, as with every witness for the State, questioned her first and Kluge's cross-examination came second. After the swearing in and introductions to the court, Basinger began by asking Hope what her relationship had been with Kenny.

'Just friends,' she replied.

Basinger then quickly moved on to questions regarding Kenny's relationship with Candy, up to June the twenty-fourth.

Hope said, 'Once in a while, Kenny said it was getting a little too thick – Candy was getting a little too possessive over him and things like that.'

Asked if the subject of marriage arose between Candy and Kenny, Hope said, 'Kenny said that he would never get married.'

Regarding Candy and Kenny's relationship during the week after the John Butler fight, preceding the fire, Hope said, 'Sometimes they would get along and sometimes they acted sick of each other.'

'And when Mike Nichols went with Candy on the twenty-ninth?' Hope was asked.

'He acted like it didn't bother him – that it was OK.'

In cross-examination, Kluge asked, 'Now, did you ever observe Mr Richey in any way make a hostile statement against Candy Barchet?'

'Not really.'

'How about on the twenty-ninth?'

'No.'

'How about the early morning hours of June thirtieth? Did he ever threaten Candy Barchet?'

'Not that I heard.'

'Did he ever make any threatening remarks about any building going to burn or anything like that?'

'Not that I heard.'

Taking into account that Kenny and Hope spent a lot of time together, as well as with others at the apartment complex, one would think that, if Kenny carried an axe for Candy, Hope would have detected something.

CANDY BARCHET

Candy strutted into the courtroom and sashayed along the aisle as if she thought she was a star preparing to perform on stage. Like Hope, she wore tight jeans and a blouse. She smirked at Kenny after she took the stand.

Basinger asked what Kenny's feelings were towards her during the first week of their relationship.

'Well, he said he loved me a lot.'

Basinger stepped back as if astonished. 'Did he say that frequently?'

'Yes, he did.'

'Daily?'

'Yeah.'

'Did he ever talk about marriage?'

'No.'

Basinger frowned. 'Uh, you're sure about that?'

'Yeah.'

'Alright.' He paused. 'Did he say anything about other guys or if he saw you with other guys?'

'Yeah. He said he'd been screwed around by a lot of girls and that, if he caught me messing around behind his back, he would kill the guy.'

'When did the defendant tell you that he'd kill the other person?'

'This was about a week after I met him.'

Kenny claims that he did say that he would hurt anyone who harmed Candy and that he only said this when consoling her after her ex-boyfriend slapped her. That was about a week after she arrived at the apartment complex.

Basinger said, 'What else did he say to you, if anything?'

'That's all I can remember.'

'Did he say anything about the other people you were with?'

'Yes, he said, "If I catch you, that's it."'

Basinger nodded. 'What did he mean by that?'

'Well, he said he would kill them.'

'That he would kill any other guys you were with?'

'Yes, sir.'

'How many times did he tell you that?'

'Frequently.'

'That week before the fire, how many times did he tell you that?'

'Not as much because that's when I told him we could remain friends but, as for anything else, there was nothing to it.'

Of course, this claim contradicted her earlier testimony in which she'd said that their parting had been mutually agreed and that they'd remained on good terms. Also, if Kenny made the threats that no one else heard, why would he continue the threats after they'd both decided it would be for the best if they parted?

'OK,' Basinger continued, 'did the sexual relationship stop?'

'Yes, it did.'

Candy went on to say that Kenny made the threat to 'kill other guys' four times in the few days before their official break-up on Wednesday – the day after the John Butler fight. Candy also testified that they both went their 'separate ways' and that Kenny neither objected to this nor displayed any anger because of the split – hardly the behaviour of the possessive, love-struck young man Basinger portrayed.

In cross-examination, Kluge asked how she and Kenny had got along on the night before the fire.

Candy shrugged. 'We didn't say nothin' to each other except for when I had given Cynthia a bath and put her pyjamas on and he passed me in the hall when he was going to the bathroom.'

'Oh, you gave her a bath and put her pyjamas on that night?'

'Yes, I did.'

Even with this minor matter Candy couldn't tell the truth. Peggy Price, supported by the testimony of others, swore that *she* was the person who had bathed Cynthia. She said, 'Candy never bothered to go in and wash her or anything. So I went in and washed her up and put her pyjamas on her. I was the one that put her to bed and kissed her goodnight and everything.'

'Well, anyway,' Kluge said, 'so, during the night of the party, he didn't do anything or say anything that would indicate to you that he was mad or angry?'

'No.'

'Didn't threaten you in any way?'

'No.'

'At any time prior to the time you retired to your apartment with Mr Nichols, did you have occasion to hear Mr Richey threaten to bomb A-building or anything?'

'No, I did not.'

PEGGY PRICE

Peggy shuffled into the courtroom wearing too much make-up and a lightweight floral dress that hung from her bulky frame like a tablecloth. She too avoided Kenny's eyes when she sat to testify.

Asked if Kenny told her of his feelings for Candy during the first week of the relationship, Peggy said, 'He told me he loved Candy and wanted to marry her.'

'When did he tell you that?' Basinger said.

'A few days after he met her.'

'All right, within a few days he said he wanted to marry her?'

'Uh-hum.'

Not only does Kenny vehemently deny this, it is also contrary to the testimonies of both Hope and Candy.

Regarding the relationship, Peggy went on to state that, during the first week Kenny met Candy, he had said that, if anybody hurt her, he would kill them. Initially, Peggy swore that Kenny made this statement a few days after Candy's ex-boyfriend slapped her but she later changed her testimony, swearing instead that 'it was the night that her ex-boyfriend, her son's father, had been there'. In other words, it was at the time when Kenny was consoling her following the assault.

In the week leading up to the fire, Peggy claimed, '[Kenny] always told me that he loved Candy and wanted to marry her.'

'OK,' Basinger said, nodding, 'and that continued the second week, after the incident with John Butler?'

'Yes,' Peggy replied.

'On how many occasions did he tell you that – express his feelings for Candy Barchet?'

'Well, he would come up every day and we would drink coffee or listen to records or else we would go over to Hope's and he would tell me he loved her and that he was going to

105

marry her someday.'

And this was the woman whose statement Basinger relied on to indict Kenny – the same woman who would later admit she lied on the stand and admit that she only told Basinger what she thought he wanted to hear.

ANALYSIS

In digging through the inconsistencies, it seems apparent that Candy's claim that Kenny threatened to kill anyone he found her with was a lie. After all, not a single person heard the threats and nor did she confide in any one of them, as a person would be apt to do. In any case, even if he had made such threats, he hadn't carried them out when the situation with John Butler had arisen – despite the fact that a knife was dangling from his belt at the time.

Also, several witnesses swore that Kenny's break-up with Candy didn't seem to bother him. This knocks a gaping hole through the State's theory of motive.

HOPE COLLINS (again)

Evidence of Hope's dishonesty appeared when she was asked if she had used drugs before the fire.

'Not that I recall,' she claimed.

Yet, during subsequent questioning over her use of drugs, she said, 'I hit it about twice.' – 'it' being a hash pipe.

Also, when questioned if there had ever been petrol in the flat, she said, 'No.'

'Paint thinner?'

'No.'

'Did you ever know of anybody using petrol or paint thinner

in the apartment?' Kluge asked.

'No.'

'During that period of two-and-a-half years you lived in the apartment, you never knew of anybody to have those items in your apartment?'

'No.'

This, of course, contradicted the information offered by Merrian Blye who Kluge inexplicably failed to call to the stand.

Kluge asked Hope if she knew Becky Leader? She claimed she didn't until Kluge reminded her that Ms Leader had worked for the Putnam County Children's Services. He asked why Ms Leader called on her a second time.

'Because somebody said I was giving [Cynthia] drugs.'

'You, of course, would never do that?'

'No, I would not.'

'You never gave her a sleeping pill?'

'No, I did not.'

'A half a sleeping pill?'

'No, I did not.'

Later, she changed her testimony when asked if she had ever given Cynthia any type of prescription drug or controlled substance. 'One time,' she said.

'You gave her adult prescribed medication?'

'Yes.'

'Did you admit that to Ms Leader when she talked to you?'

'No.'

'So you lied to her?'

'Yes.'

'But everything you've told this court is true?'

'Yes.'

Kluge asked about the situation with the babysitting. 'Did you ask Kenny to watch your daughter?'

Hope said, 'I don't remember exactly how I asked him or if he volunteered it – I don't remember.'

'Well, I'm going to ask you to think very carefully. Did you ask him to watch your daughter or, as you earlier testified, did he say he would watch her if you let him sleep on your couch?'

'I'm pretty sure that's the way it was.'

'Which? That he would watch her if you would let him sleep on the couch?'

'Yes.'

Yet, Hope's claim that she asked Kenny to watch Cynthia while in the presence of Dennis Smith and Todd Ellerbrook was not supported by either of these witnesses.

Hope went on to reaffirm that she had no knowledge of petrol or paint thinner ever being in her apartment. She did admit that paint had been spilt on the living-room carpet twice, supporting what Merrian Blye had said, but she claimed that she cleaned them using just soap and water.

Then, during Hope's testimony, a significant fact emerged – one that cast reasonable doubt on whether the fire was caused by arson. Kluge said, 'Have you ever on occasion smelled a burning smell in your apartment?'

'Yes.'

'On how many occasions?'

'Two or three.'

'When was that – in relation to the fire in which your daughter died?'

'I'm not sure how long ago the first one was but the second one was the worst and that was probably six weeks maybe.'

'Only six weeks before the fire?'

'At the latest. I mean, it could be like three to six weeks.'

'Describe to the court what you sensed at the time.'

'It smelt like hot plastic burning.'

'Burning smell?'

'Just like hot plastic. It didn't smell like it was burning, it just smelt like it was hot but there was thin-like smoke.'

Hope elaborated. 'I had just got up and I hadn't smoked a cigarette or nothin' so I knew that there was no reason for smoke. So I went to the kitchen to see if there was anything turned on and there wasn't. So I got Peggy Price and said, "Come here and smell this." And she came over and smelled it.'

Hope stated that she then spoke to the complex manager, who called the fire chief – the man who concluded that the fire had been caused by an electrical fault. Though not revealed at trial, the call was the second made to the fire chief and it resulted in his second visit to the Collinses' apartment. Both occasions had been for the plastic-burning smell accompanied by smoke. Each time the fire chief checked the apartment, he was unable to locate the source of the problem. 'Bad ventilation,' he concluded.

His conclusion, however, doesn't explain the cause of the problem. Bad ventilation doesn't cause the smell of burning plastic – nor does it account for the smoke. Was it possible that the smoke came from an appliance or faulty electrical wiring? Were the burning smell and the smoke warning signs of a fire about to happen?

Eventually, Kluge asked Hope the same question he posed to every witness who attended the party. 'During the period on the twenty-ninth, when you sat on the steps with the others, did you hear Kenny say anything to the effect that A-building was going to burn tonight?'

And Hope gave the same answer as every witness who had sat on the steps. 'No.'

Only Peggy Price, Bob Dannenberg and Shirley Baker claimed that Kenny made this threat – or a variation of it – and all three of them swore that he had made the threat later in the evening and inside Peggy's apartment.

The reason Kluge questioned the witnesses about whether Kenny made a threat on the steps was to prove that, again, another witness lied. This damaging witness was a seventy-year-old by the name of Juanita Altimus.

JUANITA ALTIMUS

If appearances were anything to go by, few would dispute the honesty of Juanita Altimus. She stepped carefully into the courtroom and moved slowly along the aisle, looking as fragile as a grandmother in the final days of her life. It took her some time to finally reach the stand and then climb on to the seat. During the subsequent questioning, Judge Corrogan had to ask her to speak up.

Sometimes, in well-publicised cases, witnesses pop up and volunteer information that they swear is first-hand knowledge but, in reality, it is gossip or a creation of their own imaginations. Often they are motivated by wanting to be in the limelight. Juanita Altimus could have been just such an attention seeker. Her daughter, some years later, would betray her mother's trust by confiding in someone that her mother had lied on the stand. Yet, this was hardly a startling new revelation.

At trial, one witness, Sherry Tice, testified that Ms Altimus often gossiped at the apartment complex and that a person had to be sceptical about the stories she told as she had the reputation of habitually lying.

Ms Altimus quickly revealed this trait in court when she claimed that a 'bunch of people' sat on the southside steps of the breezeway when, in fact, they had been sitting on the northside steps. She identified the 'bunch of people' as including Candy – Ms Altimus lived across from Candy's apartment – Kenny, Hope, Peggy, Bob and John. But John had not been present and hadn't returned to the apartment complex since his fight with Kenny.

'What were they doing?' Basinger asked.

'Raising the devil for one thing,' Ms Altimus replied, looking indignant.

Basinger stepped closer to the stand. 'What do you mean by that?'

'They were drinking and talking loud and vulgar. They must have been smoking marijuana because it was sure strong whatever it was.'

The only smoking of drugs had been in Hope's apartment and that was later that evening.

'You smelled what seemed to be marijuana to you?'

'Yes.'

'Have you smelled marijuana before?'

'It burned my nose and eyes and I had to shut my front door. It was coming down to my apartment.'

Of course, the breezeway was an open stair and any slight wind would have passed right through, taking any smell with it.

'What else happened late in the afternoon, that evening?'

'It seems like Richey was mad about something because he came down the steps and he was on the lower part of the steps and he said, "A-building is going to burn tonight!"'

Ms Altimus then explained that she had stood near the door of her apartment, about ten feet from Kenny. 'What I could understand the most was, when he wasn't yellin', was that he was arguing with somebody. I think it was one of the men.'

'What happened? What did he say?' Basinger pressed.

'That's when he hollered that A-building was going to burn tonight.'

At first, Ms Altimus testified that no one else was around when Kenny 'hollered' the threat but then she said seven or eight people were sitting a few steps up from him when the threat was made. She then swore that she felt scared by the threat and she retreated to her apartment and closed her door. Not one person even recalled seeing the old woman on the evening in question.

'What happened next?' Basinger said.

'Well, they just hung around out there and finally, if I'm not mistaken, Hope left and the rest of them went wherever they was going to go and Richey was supposed to have been there, as far as I could make out, with Cynthia, the baby.'

Of course, how she witnessed this when, by her own admission, she was in her apartment with her door closed remains a mystery.

'What time did you go to bed that night?'

'About ten thirty.'

This was many hours before people dispersed from the party.

In cross-examination, Kluge asked her how she reached the conclusion that Kenny was supposed to have been babysitting Cynthia.

'Well,' Ms Altimus said, 'he stayed with Hope and sometimes he babysitted (sic) Cynthia and I seen him up on the patio earlier.'

Even if she could manage the impossible of seeing Kenny on Hope's balcony from her apartment, she didn't explain how she came to the conclusion that Kenny's presence there meant that he was babysitting Cynthia.

Ms Altimus had also told Basinger that, at noon on June the thirtieth, when a smoking chair flew out of Hope's balcony window, Kenny leaned against Candy's shed and said, 'It looks like I did a hell of a good job, don't it?'

However, at noon on June the thirtieth, Police Chief Miller and Sergeant Stechschulte had entered Dad's apartment and wakened Kenny from a 'heavy sleep' to question him, as Stechschulte testified. Kenny could not have been leaning against the shed at this time as Ms Altimus stated.

She changed her story when Kluge pointed this fact out to her. Adamantly, she then told Kluge that the incident must have happened at noon on July the first rather than June the thirtieth. This is even more ridiculous. Not only was Kenny having his cast changed twenty-six miles away at the Lima medical centre but the fire had gutted the apartment the day before and under no circumstances would a smoking chair, which would have constituted a fire hazard, have been left in the apartment overnight.

Furthermore, if Ms Altimus had overheard Kenny saying something as evil and incriminating as admitting he started the fire, wouldn't she, like any reasonable person, have instantly reported it to a police officer, many of whom were still in the vicinity? It was four days after the fire before Ms Altimus contacted the police, when a frenzy of gossip had already engulfed the complex.

When Kluge asked her why she had failed to report Kenny's alleged statement to a police officer, she claimed, 'Maybe it's because I'm an old woman and I didn't think of it or maybe I just . . . I didn't think of it.'

MIKE NICHOLS

Mike Nichols plodded into the courtroom, eyes flitting about, wearing the same suit he had worn to his brother's wedding some months before. He self-consciously smoothed down his receding dark hair as he took the stand. During the ensuing questioning, he frequently shifted around in his seat.

He testified that, after the firemen settled Kenny down, Kenny approached him. 'Me and Candy was standing outside, out front on the lawn, and that's when Kenny came down there and looked at me and he said a couple of words to Candy which I can't remember. He said, then looked at me (sic) and he said, "Well," he says (sic), "why don't we finish it now since you think you're so bad?"'

'How soon after the fire was out did he say that?' Basinger asked.

'OK, they was still trying to get it out.'

During cross-examination, Kluge said, 'Before you saw him out on the lawn after the fire, on any other occasions, had Kenny ever threatened you or in any way made you believe he was out to harm Candy?'

'No, he did not – just when he said that.'

'That was the only time?'

'That was it.'

SHIRLEY BAKER

Shirley Baker entered the courtroom and hurried to the stand as if she wanted to get things over with as quickly as possible. She wore pink polyester trousers and a white untucked shirt with red and yellow flowers covering its front and back.

The judges would rely on Shirley Baker's short testimony and the prosecution would forever after cast her as a witness who definitively reported that she heard Kenny state that 'the building is going to burn'. However, Shirley Baker actually recounted gossip. Regarding this gossip and what the police made of it, Ms Baker testified, 'Yeah, they would put words . . . the words that we would put out – they would change the words. You know how people will turn things around? I do believe that's what they did on quite a few of the conversations that were made.'

Kluge pressed her, saying, 'One of the main things that has come out of this trial is the phrase that Kenny had used on that night – that he was going to burn A-building down or that the building was going to burn. Did you hear him say that?'

Ms Baker shook her head. 'I personally did not hear him say that. I heard them – people – repeating that to me. That's what I heard.'

'But you never heard Kenny Richey say that he was going to

burn A-building?' Kluge asked.

'I did not, no. I did not,' Ms Baker replied.

As Kenny listened to Shirley Baker and Mike Nichols and all the witnesses before him, he remembered wishing he had a pair of Wellington boots because the shit was getting deep. He only hoped that the judges would remember the testimony of the police officers, all of whom swore that he had been immediately placed in custody when he was escorted from the breezeway, and that they would take into account Shirley Baker's testimony regarding the nature of the gossip and the exaggeration and twisting of words.

FIRE MARSHAL CRYER

Fire Marshal Cryer was a short, stout man and he climbed to the stand wearing a dark suit with a large knotted tie. He hardly looked impressive but his testimony was to deliver such a blow that the defence never recovered from it. This should not have been the case – any lawyer who had done his research could have torched the fire marshal's theory.

He began his testimony by giving details of his experience with fires which dated back to 1943. His coverage of this filled ten pages of the court reporter's transcript. Basinger impressed on the judges that here sat a fire expert who knew what he was talking about – so do not try to question or dispute what he says. And, regrettably, Kluge did not.

Basinger asked Cryer about what he observed upon arriving at the apartment.

'Well,' Cryer said, 'when I arrived at the fire scene, I observed that we had a real intense fire. I observed that the door, the metal entrance door, was warped, which (sic) takes a lot of heat to warp a metal entrance door. I also observed that it came out of the sliding balcony patio door, the heat did. It was so intense that it come (*sic*) right up and around over the roof and it also burned the railing on the patio on the second floor there.'

'Alright,' Basinger said. 'Can you tell us what you observed about the balcony itself?'

Cryer's verbatim reply was, 'Well, the balcony was burnt from about three foot up. It was burnt real deep, real intense heat. The lower part of the balcony, there wasn't too much heat in areas and then other areas there was burns down between the wood decking which looked very suspicious at the time because we know fire goes up, burns up – heat goes up – and why there would be burns in between the wood decking indicated to me that there was an accelerant used.'

If, when he first saw the fire scene, Cryer did believe that an accelerant had been used, then why did it take him until July the seventeenth to take a sample of the balcony wood?

Judge Abood stopped Basinger in order to ask precisely this question.

Cryer answered, 'I just didn't think about that being a trailer (*sic*) [of accelerants] out there and being connected with it at first. I was concentrating on the living-room area more and I just didn't think about that being a good source as far as finding an accelerant. I really didn't think I would find an accelerant there.'

By his own admission, this means he spent seventeen days concentrating on the living-room area before he finally took a sample from the balcony.

Next, Basinger asked Cryer when he had reached the conclusion that accelerants were splashed on the balcony.

'I reached that conclusion about the second day I was on the fire scene and we started getting things cleaned off.'

In view of what he'd just said, this made little sense. Cryer also swore that the complex owner gutted the apartment and cleaned the floors and walls, allegedly unbeknownst to him, on the day of the fire. This would have left nothing for Cryer to 'clean off'. And, again, if he reached his conclusion on the second day after the fire, why did he wait until July the seventeenth to take any samples?

A blown-up picture slide of the balcony was exhibited to the court. Cryer explained, 'This here is the patio balcony after the railing had been removed and it shows the burn which runs along there and even in the crack there which indicates that there is an accelerant there. That's the only way you would get a burn down in there like that.'

Yet, the sample taken from this charred area tested negative for the presence of accelerants.

Cryer continued with little encouragement from Basinger. 'There is an accelerant used on this fire. It was either throwed (sic) in from the patio area or else it was poured in and a trailer run out on to the patio area to ignite the fire.'

Basinger nodded. He said, 'I would like you to list the reasons of those conclusions for the use of accelerants.'

'We had pour patterns,' Cryer said. 'In other words, it is just like if you take and pour water on the top of a desk, the water will seep to low levels and that's the same way flammable liquids do and you will get burns just like that. If it would not have been a flammable liquid, the fire would not have burnt as intense (sic) and quickly as it did.'

Another of many slides passed before the court. Cryer explained, 'This shows the patio balcony and it shows the storage building (tool shed) under there (Hope's balcony) and how close it is [to the balcony]. It is easy to get up from the storage building. You can jump up there, climb up yourself. You can stand there (on the roof of the shed) and you have got about three feet over to this area here (the balcony edge). So it would be very easy to get access to the patio balcony with the storage building (tool shed) sitting there (underneath the balcony).'

They soon focused on the carpet which was of a sponge rubber type.

'In the centre of the room, again the carpet was completely gone?' Basinger said, splaying his hands out before him.

'Yes, sir,' Cryer replied.

It was a speculative answer because part of this section of the carpet could have been left at the dump and Cryer had taken no pictures of the carpet while it lay in Hope's apartment. If he had believed that the fire was suspicious, wouldn't he have taken photographs of the carpet at the fire scene?

Cryer said that he attributed the hole in the carpet to be where an accelerant had been poured, causing it to burn more intensely at that point.

'To burn all the way through to the concrete?' Basinger expanded.

'Yes, it did in a lot of areas.'

They then moved their focus to the smoke detector. It had been found hanging on its wires from where it was mounted on the ceiling. Initially, Cryer told the court, 'I feel quite certain that smoke detector was pulled down.' But, later, he said, 'Very intense heat and flame caused [the smoke detector] to melt down.'

Cryer made several changes in his testimony throughout the proceedings and a good argument could be made that he perjured himself. After he swore that he never stated a fire was arson until he received his lab reports, Kluge countered, 'Well, you stated that, of course, the next day, July first, you testified you stated that [your conclusion that the fire was arson] to Mr Basinger.'

'No,' Cryer replied, folding his arms across his chest.

However, at Kenny's preliminary trial, Cryer had testified, 'OK, I talked to the assistant prosecutor later on in the afternoon [of July first], I think it was around three o'clock or something like that.'

'So you advised Mr Basinger that you believed it to be arson – is that correct?' Kluge said.

Kenny Richey aged 4 and younger brother Tom aged 2, at home in Edinburgh, Scotland.

The Richey boys – Kenny aged 7, Tom aged 4 and Steven aged eighteen months – playing outside their Edinburgh tenement flat.

A young Kenny,
sporting his first
moustache, relaxes at
home after a busy
day at work.

Kenny with parents
Eileen and Jim in
1982.

A new life in America and a new career in the US Marines' 1st Recon Company. Early days in dress uniform (left) and, below, a more confident Kenny, now an experienced soldier.

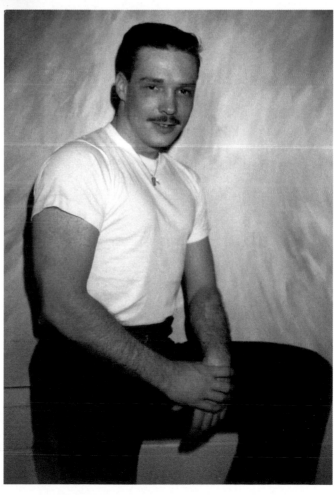

Kenny and Wendy on their wedding day in 1984, with Eileen, Jim, Tom and Steven.

Kenny Richey's crest, a symbol of the hope that, one day, he could return to Scotland.

Kenny Richey behind the bars of the cell where he would spend nearly twenty years of his life.

DEATH
ROW

Behind this steel door
is the grim reality of
life on death row.

Eileen Richey with her photos of Kenny (left) and Tom. Two of her three sons have been in US jails for nearly twenty years.

Clive Stafford-Smith, the international human rights lawyer who helped Kenny find a top-quality legal team to secure his release.

Karen Torley who has campaigned tirelessly for Kenny's release. She runs his website www.kennyrichey.org from her home in Cambuslang, Glasgow.

Karen meets Kenny's son, Sean, who Kenny hasn't seen since Sean was a baby.

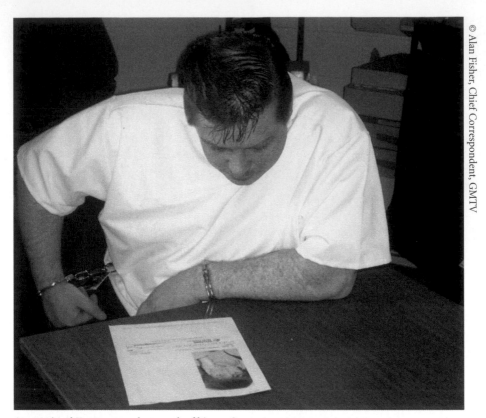

An emotional Kenny sees a photograph of his son Sean.

Kenny's brother Tom Richey, author, and their dad, Jim Richey.

Kenny Richey – still shackled and still waiting to be released from death row.

'Yes, sir,' Cryer said.

'So you did tell Mr Basinger that he could authorise arson charges?'

'Yes. I told him it was definitely an arson case.'

Why Kluge failed to request the court to impeach Cryer for this is another example of bad lawyering.

ANALYSIS

In the 1952 case, *Winterich v. State of Ohio* the court declared that a 'defendant in a criminal action cannot be convicted on general principles or mere suspicion and, in order to convict, it is essential that all material elements of the offence charged be proven beyond a reasonable doubt'.

There was easily enough evidence and contradiction during Kenny's trial to clearly establish reasonable doubt.

Despite all the testimonial and circumstantial material evidence, the court was no closer to the truth of what happened from the moment Kenny stepped out of Donna Michaels' view at approximately 3.40 a.m. until approximately 4.30 a.m. (fifteen minutes after the first call was received by the fire department) when Kenny hurried past Sandra Spencer and her children, as he headed for the burning apartment. Because Kenny was the accused, his account of his movements carried little weight. Only the facts, then, can be relied on. The court calls this process 'weighing of the evidence'.

Most people are familiar with the scales of justice and the status of the blindfolded woman holding the scales in one hand, a sword in the other. The statue is a symbol of both the American and the British judicial system but few understand its symbolism – the woman represents the court and the sword represents the power and authority of the court; the scales represent a base for both parties to present their evidence, the facts; and the blindfold means she, the court, is blind to all evidence not presented. The party that presents the heaviest, strongest evidence is the side that outweighs the other, tipping the scales of justice and thereby winning the decision. But, in Kenny's case, it appears the scales were unfairly balanced from the outset.

The prosecution's theory was weak.

The first discrepancy exists at the beginning. McAdam's Commercial Greenhouse did stock petrol and paint thinner but the cans were some distance from each other. It makes little sense that Kenny would stagger over to the petrol cans, lift one and then stagger over to the cans of paint thinner and lift one of those. Wouldn't an arsonist just lift two of either of the flammables from the nearest stack?

Also, Kenneth Wright, the greenhouse owner could not confirm that any of his stock had been stolen. He testified that, to the best of his knowledge, 'no accelerants were missing' and no empty containers were ever recovered. But let's say that Kenny did procure the accelerants from the greenhouse or from elsewhere. He had broken his hand one week before and was wearing a temporary cast. A temporary cast is more disabling than a full cast because it provides less protection and less support for the broken bone. You can't place much pressure on the hand, especially not body weight. The unbroken fingers can be used in a limited fashion to write or eat with utensils. Candy Barchet, in fact, testified that she observed Kenny using his fingers to hold a fork – a detail that the prosecution had, at one point, opposed, claiming that he could barely hold a pen. The fact is that even an experienced cat burglar would have difficulty maintaining silence while climbing up and down Hope's balcony with cans of accelerants. It is improbable Kenny could make the climb on to a sloping shed roof while carrying containers with a broken hand and while drunk – let alone make such a climb in silence.

Mike Nichols testified that he was a light sleeper. When asked if someone had jumped from Hope's balcony on to the roof of the shed would he be able to hear from Candy's bedroom, he said, 'Yes.' Neither he nor Candy heard a sound.

Furthermore, why would Kenny climb the balcony when an easier form of entry into the apartment beckoned through an unlocked front door?

Let's assume he did use the front door to enter the apartment. After dousing the living room and the balcony with petrol and paint thinner, he would still have had to escape down the breezeway stairs, with empty cans, in silence.

Cryer claimed the indication that petrol and paint thinner were poured and splashed in the living room and balcony was apparent. Yet, it was known that Kenny had been so blitzed from the party, he collapsed in some bushes for several minutes before he got up and staggered out of Donna Michaels' view. Isn't it reasonable to believe that accelerants would've spattered on to his boots and clothing? And how would it be possible for anyone to avoid absorbing traces of chemicals on their clothing by 'after touches' or by contact with the containers while carrying them?

Dan Gelphius, a forensic chemist for the Ohio State Arson Crime Laboratory tested Kenny's boots. Extensive tests were conducted. The forensic chemist soaked the articles with diethyl ether anhydrous. He allowed this liquid to drip into vials then concentrated it to a volume of one hundred microlitres where he then analysed them on a gas chromatograph. He testified, 'The findings indicative of gas chromatic analysis failed to reveal the presence of accelerants.' He elaborated, explaining that, in testing the boots, he completely covered them with diethyl ether anhydrous and, had there been a speck of petrol or paint thinner, its presence would have been detected. It is difficult to swallow the theory that Kenny could splash accelerants without spattering one speck somewhere on to his clothing.

A drunken person, handicapped by a cast on his hand, would have been hard pressed to carry a couple of containers of flammables up to an apartment. But this feat would have been all the more difficult if not impossible if that person also has not to get a single drop of petrol or paint thinner on his clothing and then has to dispose of the incriminating containers. What is equally troubling is the time span involved. From the time Kenny stepped out of Donna Michaels' view (3.40 a.m.) until the first call to the fire department (4.15 a.m.) was made, thirty five minutes elapsed. A fully fit, sober person would be hard pushed to do this within the time.

The living-room carpet samples and the woodchip sample from the balcony were the only sources that tested positive for the trace of flammables. The paint thinner sample from the balcony deck was prised off an unburned area, from a small spot that was darker in colour than the surrounding wood. Cryer theorised it was evidence of a splash of flammable that had failed to catch fire. His theory is improbable.

Cryer said he prised the sample from deep in the decking. With this in mind, one must also consider that the balcony, built entirely of wood, was weather treated. It takes a substantial amount of time for an accelerant to penetrate deeply into treated wood, to pass through its weather shield. Cryer himself confirmed this fact during the trial. 'That there (on the balcony deck) is a treated wood which won't absorb like your open green wood would.'

The time that elapsed from the moment Kenny could have splashed the deck with paint thinner to the time a fireman's hose shot water over the burning deck, washing it, amounted to around an hour – not long enough for an accelerant to be absorbed deeply into the wood. Additionally, if Kenny had splashed flammables over the balcony, the flammables would have dripped through the half-inch space that separated each board of the balcony deck. Cryer did check the underside of the deck for accelerant traces and he checked the concrete of Candy Barchet's patio directly below Hope's balcony. No traces of accelerants were detected – not even a droplet. It is impossible to splash a deck that has half-inch spaces between each deck board without one drop falling below.

But how can the presence of paint thinner on the deck be accounted for? The apartment complex was over ten years old. Hope's apartment had probably worn a few coats of paint in its lifetime. It's logical that, during one or more of these paint jobs, paint cans, paint brushes, paint thinner and other paraphernalia were placed outside on the balcony deck to minimise the build-up of fumes in the badly ventilated apartment. The painter probably soaked his brushes in a solution of paint thinner and the soaking brushes wouldn't be left inside the apartment if they didn't have to be. The painter would naturally set them outside on the balcony. It's conceivable that, on one occasion, paint thinner was set on the deck and contamination occurred, either from a spill or, more likely, when a soaking brush was removed from the container of paint thinner. Supporting this theory is the fact that the positive woodchip sample that Cryer had obtained was only four inches from the outer edge of the balcony. It's a location where soaking brushes and the like would sensibly be placed – out of the way against the edge of the deck where they would be less likely to be knocked over.

Then the question of evaporation arises. If paint thinner had dripped on to the deck and been absorbed into the wood, would it evaporate over the years? Cryer answered this while answering an unrelated question. He said, 'Our lab has taken pine boards or pine rafters out of houses that were a hundred years old and extracted turpentine out of it (sic). So, it is not impossible – once something is in there, it is pretty probable a good lab will find it.'

It's also pretty probable that the paint thinner his lab extracted from the balcony woodchip wasn't splashed on the balcony by an arsonist. This is supported by the finding that no flammable hydrocarbons were found in the samples taken from the charred area of the balcony deck. Kluge questioned the fire marshal about this charred area. 'Now, normally, and you correct me if I'm wrong, when water is put on a fire that is burned by an accelerant, it has a tendency to lock the accelerant into the substance, doesn't it?'

'Well,' Cryer replied, smiling and seeming to enjoy being the star witness, 'it just depends on what kind of material we're talking about whether it locks it in.'

'Well, how about wood?'

Cryer nodded. 'It will hold it in.'

'OK. So, then, if there were any accelerants that caused the fire in the heavy (*sic*) charred area, they would have been locked in the wood and you would have found them, right?'

Conceding nothing to the defence, Cryer said, 'No, because, as deep as that is charred and burnt there, the fire probably destroyed the accelerants in the charred area.'

Yet, during a previous recital of experiments he'd undertaken, Cryer said, 'We have run different tests with accelerants. We know accelerants will take and lie on a board and then seep down, in between the cracks of the board. And we know you can take and burn that board, set it on fire and burn it, and there will still be remains of the accelerant in the tongue and groove or where there is cracks (*sic*) and that's where it stays at.'

If flammables had been splashed on the charred area of Hope's balcony, the forensic lab should have found them, as Cryer insisted they could have. And, again, why were no traces of flammables found on the underside of the balcony or on the patio below? The obvious answer to this is that none were to be found because no flammables were splashed on the balcony.

As I read and analysed Kenny's trial transcripts, I just wasn't convinced, beyond a reasonable doubt, of Cryer's findings regarding the balcony. My scepticism only increased when I scrutinised his findings in the living room. The positive petrol and paint thinner samples on the carpet were taken within a couple of feet of each other in an area near the apartment's hallway entrance within proximity of the fire's hot-spot. The prosecution argued that these samples were positive proof that Kenny poured flammables over the living room. However, the theory defies common sense. If Cryer's testimony was correct, it would be impossible for any raw accelerant to have survived in the carpet so close to the hot-spot.

The balcony fire, being outside, could never have been as hot as the inferno within the enclosed walls of the apartment. Cryer testified that no flammables could be detected in the charred wood of the balcony deck because the fire was so intense that it burned all traces of hydrocarbons. If true, then how would it be possible for flammable hydrocarbons to survive in a fibre more flammable than wood, inside the apartment where it was much hotter? It was a contradiction in Cryer's theory that Kluge failed to take advantage of.

The petrol and paint thinner must have come from a different source.

The carpet and debris from the apartment had been thrown on to the bed of a lorry and transported to the county dump. The carpet lay under accumulated rubbish until the afternoon of July the first, when deputies retrieved it. As Deputy Berger testified, 'We dug it up, drug it out and took it to the sheriff's department.'

Kluge asked, 'The way the garbage was stacked on top of the carpet, is it conceivable that other types of liquid might have absorbed into that carpet out at the dump?'

'At the dump, possibly, yes, it's possible,' Deputy Berger said.

Until July the twenty-first the carpet lay unrolled, drying on the concrete forecourt of the police station. For nearly three weeks the carpet lay there, near petrol pumps used by police vehicles. Before Fire Marshal Cryer cut samples from it, it is possible that petrol hydrocarbons contaminated the evidence. Some years later, Sergeant Stechschulte did, in fact, admit this to a reporter who was investigating the case. He said, 'It was a mistake laying that carpet out in front of the gasoline pumps.'

The positive results from the carpet were unreliable due to the mishandling of evidence. Kluge prodded Cryer for confirmation of this fact but Cryer grinned, saying, 'I can't say that it wouldn't and I can't say that it would.'

So, had the flammables come from the dump and the parking lot or did they come from a different source?

Could the flammables have come from Hope cleaning up a paint spill or from her husband's routine of using petrol to clean car parts in the living room? As Cryer testified, the hydrocarbons of an accelerant will remain in something indefinitely. The hydrocarbons from previously spilled accelerants could have survived the inferno in the apartment.

The fire's hot-spot, stretching from the balcony door to one corner of the hallway entrance, completely burned the carpet, leaving a large bald spot and a couple of unconnected bald spots. Cryer claimed these spots were signs of accelerant use – pour patterns. However, a square of the carpet that had been protected by the television stand was tested to see if it continued burning by itself after being touched by a match. It did. Cryer said, 'It continued to burn after the source of the fire was taken away from it.' The carpet, then, could burn without the aid of accelerants.

The bald spots where the carpet had burned away completely left the concrete floor of the apartment exposed. Kluge had asked Cryer to verify if concrete absorbs accelerants.

'Yes,' Cryer replied.

'OK,' Kluge said, 'now you've got a fire scene. The day after the fire, you suspect it was arson. You don't have the carpet because the carpet is out at the dump and, by this time, the whole living room has been cleaned, right?'

'Yes, sir.'

'Everything is out of the apartment. Do you go back a day after the fire and take samples of the cement floor at all?'

'No, sir. No, sir.'

'Is there a reason for that?'

'Very, very rarely do we ever take samples of a cement floor because it is tough to get and the lab don't like to run it and, because there was no discolouration, there was no indication that there would be anything there.'

The fire marshal then claimed that flammables never could have touched the cement because the carpet acted like a blotter, holding the flammables in. Logically, the carpet would act like a blotter or sponge but, even so, a liquid would still wet the surface of the cement underneath and, in turn, it would be absorbed into the concrete.

Two areas of the carpet tested positive for flammables so Kluge asked Cryer if he took samples of the cement under those areas because, had the concrete samples tested negative, then the evidence would have suggested that the carpet was contaminated after its removal from the apartment.

'No sir,' Cryer said.

'Was there a reason for that?' Kluge said.

'We seldom take samples on cement,' Cryer repeated and explained that there would be no point in taking a sample of the concrete if a sample had been taken of the rug. 'If nothing showed on the carpeting, there certainly wasn't going to be anything on the concrete underneath.'

'But there was accelerant revealed [in the carpet], right?'

'Yes, but I didn't know that at the time.'

'I understand,' Kluge said. 'But, after you discovered that there was, did you go back and take a sample?'

'No,' Cryer replied.

But, on July the seventeenth, Cryer did return to the apartment to take a sample of the concrete floor. He took concrete chips from an area where the fan had sat. Again contradicting himself, he explained why he took a sample from this particular spot. 'If there would have been any accelerant in the cement there would have been a discolouration. That's the reason I took it where I took it – because there was a discolouration in the concrete and there was a crack in the concrete.'

'What do you attribute that to?' Kluge countered.

'I attribute that to an accelerant or liquid of some type poured on the floor.'

These concrete chips tested negative for flammables yet Kluge failed to have Cryer explain why, despite the fact that Cryer had stated that concrete would absorb even the most miniscule amount of accelerant. Presumably, like his balcony theory, he would have said that the super-hot fire burned all traces of accelerant absorbed by the concrete. Again, such a theory would support the fact that, only several feet away, no raw accelerant in the carpet could have survived the blaze.

Kluge was simply out of his depth as a criminal trial lawyer. Of all his blunders, the most glaring had to involve Gregory Dubois, who Kluge retained to conduct an independent investigation of the fire. Kluge had contacted CTL Engineering who claimed they had experts in the field of arson investigation. They sent Gregory Dubois to Putnam County. Dubois' education was limited to a bachelor's degree in metallurgical engineering and a partially completed stint in business school. Although accredited in Ohio as an accident reconstructionist, he primarily performed 'vehicle accident reconstructions'. He had no accreditations in arson or fire investigations. In fact, although Dubois was a member of the International Association of Arson Investigators (IAAI), his involvement was limited to receiving quarterly publications in the mail. At the time Kluge hired Dubois, he had attended no IAAI seminars on fire investigation.

Dubois' resumé, which Kluge had received, indicated that he worked as a metallurgical engineer and that his only arson-related training consisted of two two-day courses, neither of which involved the subject of burn patterns. Both courses he attended had been taught by personnel form the Ohio State Arson Lab, the very institution whose conclusions Dubois was hired to review. Moreover, Dubois would openly admit that he admired Mohamed Gohar, chief of the Ohio State Arson Lab and the man who had overseen the testing in Kenny's case. Dubois believed that Gohar stayed at the forefront of technology and was 'quite authoritative in his field'. At the time Kluge hired him, Dubois admitted that he believed the State fire marshal's office did a better job of fire-sample analysis than his own association did.

Kluge had been appointed to represent Kenny on July the fourteenth 1986 and, although he received the Ohio State Arson Lab reports on August the fifth, he did not meet with Dubois or any other potential expert until September the eleventh 1986. At that meeting, Kluge told him that he was 'interested in keeping costs to a minimum' and he also told Dubois that he wanted about ten hours to be spent on the initial investigation. Kluge did not enquire about what type of work would be necessary to investigate the fire. According to Dubois, 'The ten hours was given to me by Kluge as an implied budget, that this was all he could afford in this particular case to have the time spent, and he wanted to know what I could do for ten hours' worth of time.'

It was not until November the eighteenth 1986, a month and a half before Kenny's trial, that Kluge contacted Dubois again. But, during that interim, Dubois had conducted no work on Kenny's case. By this point, despite having no idea what conclusions Dubois would reach, Kluge put Dubois's name on the defence's list as a witness.

When Dubois's investigation finally began, Dubois contacted Gohar who agreed to meet him. As Dubois would admit, they 'work[ed] together, went through each chromatogram and [Dubois] had [Gohar] show [him] which standard he used and which result he got and which sample matched which chromatogram'. Dubois conducted no independent testing of the samples, nor did he interview Cryer. He did not learn of such errors like the mishandling of the carpet – only that it tested positive for traces of paint thinner and petrol.

As it turned out, Kluge was not aware that Dubois had not conducted any independent testing until well after the trial. Although Kluge never asked Dubois to perform any independent testing, he would later admit that he 'assumed [Dubois] would do more than just look at [the] reports of Cryer'. Furthermore, when Dubois presented his findings to Kluge (that he didn't dispute the State's conclusion that the fire was arson), Kluge did not ask Dubois what the basis was for his findings. Dubois submitted no written report to Kluge and stated that Kluge was 'surprisingly non-argumentative with me [and] didn't challenge me on what I thought or why I thought what I did or anything'. Nor did Dubois recall Kluge ever asking him about any problems with the State's evidence.

Rather, Kluge admitted, 'Once Dubois confirmed that everything Cryer had done was accurate and appeared to be in order, we decided at that point not to use him.' Reading between the lines, Basinger then subpoenaed Dubois to testify – effectively *against* Kenny. Dubois did contact Kluge and asked for help resisting the subpoena but he received none. According to Dubois, Kluge said to him, 'You'll just have to do what you have to do.' Consequently, Kenny's sole so-called forensic expert ended up testifying against him.

At trial, Basinger asked Dubois, 'Do you agree with the conclusion that accelerants were used in the apartment of Hope Collins?'

'Based on the available evidence, yes,' Dubois replied.

Incredibly, when asked if he wished to cross-examine, Kluge said, 'Not at this time, Your Honour.'

Judge Corrigan raised his brow. 'What do you mean, "Not at this time"? Do you intend to call him?'

'We may, yes,' Kluge replied. He never did. In failing to question Dubois and show the court that the man never personally investigated the fire, Kluge essentially admitted that the defence agreed the fire had been caused by arson.

Yet, if arson did not cause the fire, what did? Two alternative possibilities exist.

Cynthia Collins had a circular burn on her wrist. It is proof that she was awake before or during the fire because flames did not enter her bedroom at the rear of the apartment. She had, therefore, to have been awake and out of the room in order to have touched something hot enough to burn her. Volunteer fireman and lead investigator, Sergeant Steve Stechschulte, found her body lying face down on the floor of her room. An autopsy revealed that she died from carbon monoxide poisoning, a lack of air. Her wrist burn, people assumed, had been caused by the hot bedroom door handle. However, this is unlikely because the shape of the door handle couldn't make a small circular burn. The face of the door handle was flat, like an orange sliced in half. It could only have made a large circular burn. The small circular burn on Cynthia's wrist had to have been caused by an object outside the room because no object in the room, other than the door handle, could have been hot because the fire did not make it as far as the room. Is it possible Cynthia burned her hand while starting the fire herself?

Although it never came out at trial, Cynthia had, on three previous occasions, started fires. The most serious of these had been on her mother's bed. As Peggy Price would later swear in an affidavit, 'Cynthia was fascinated by fire. She played with matches and lighters and used to take them from visitors and take them to her room.'

When Hope and others had been smoking drugs in the apartment about three-and-half hours before the fire, Cynthia wandered into the living room. Hope recalled Cynthia sitting on Robert Neinberg's knee for five minutes before hopping off to seek attention from Doug Mull. Smoking materials lay around. It's possible Cynthia lifted matches or a cigarette lighter. It's also possible one of those items was left behind.

Cynthia could have set fire to any object within the area of the hot-spot – a chair, the sofa, an article of clothing left on the floor – or even a match that had been dropped on to the carpet itself could've been the starting point. She could have fled in panic when she saw the flames grow out of control. Maybe she burned her wrist before fleeing or maybe she returned to the fire to try to extinguish it or save a favourite toy and, in the process, burned her wrist.

The second possible cause of the fire is that it was electrical. On two occasions, the fire chief had to be called to investigate the smell of burning plastic which was accompanied with a thin film of smoke in Hope's apartment. According to Hope's testimony, the latest of these mysterious incidents happened a matter of weeks before the fatal fire. She would later tell an investigating television reporter that both incidents actually happened within ten days of the fire.

What of the intensity of the fire, which was the first and foremost indication that the prosecution relied on to support their arson theory? They stated that, unless some kind of accelerant had been present, the fire could not have progressed so quickly in the forty-minute period before firemen arrived. But the fact is that, even without the aid of flammables, a fire can devastate a room in as little as seven minutes. Something called 'flashover' could have accounted for the quick progress of the fire.

Flashover happens when fire in an enclosed room reaches temperatures of over two thousand degrees. During flashover, hot fire gasses gather near the ceiling. These gasses radiate such heat that they cause combustible items below to burst into flames. Petroleum based products, such as plastics, melt and cause accelerant-like pour patterns.

The phenomenon was investigated in the early 1980s by researchers at the prestigious Harvard University and at the US National Bureau of Standards Center for Research. The Harvard researchers filmed a one-inch flame as it grew, without the aid of flammables, until it engulfed a room. The whole process took under seven minutes. The recognition of flashover as a possibility, especially in house fires, has changed assumptions about how fires start and progress. There is scientific agreement that it can mimic arson which, of course, means it can be mistaken for arson. It produces intense burning with signs of multiple points of ignition. Hope's poorly ventilated apartment would have provided just the right conditions for flashover to occur.

Despite swearing that only arson could account for the quick intense blaze that left deep charring and signs of multiple ignition points, it's likely that Cryer already knew of the effects of flashover at the time of Kenny's trial. It was something that fire investigators had been aware of from as far back as 1984. Kenny, however, only learned of flashover in 1990 – three years too late – when he read an article in the *Los Angeles Times* that brought flashover to the attention of the general public. The article described how, because of new evidence relating to flashover, two men received retrials in the State of California.

Finally, the most disturbing aspect of Kenny's case was not the lack of evidence or the lies or the conflicting trial testimonies or the dubious police procedures or the poor legal decisions – it was Kenny's alleged motive. Why would he start a fire upstairs in a different apartment with the intention of killing two people in an apartment below, under a concrete floor? No matter how flexible your imagination is, it is difficult to conceive how this would be possible.

If Kenny was intent on murdering Candy and Mike, wouldn't

he make the job a lot easier for himself by throwing a petrol bomb through Candy's open bedroom window? And the window had been open – Candy stated that she had kept the window open because it had been such a hot night. For Kenny to knowingly murder a child while attempting the impossible deed of killing Candy and Mike defies logic, particularly when you consider Kenny's relationship with Cynthia.

Asked if Kenny was good with children, Hope testified, 'I thought he was excellent with kids.'

'And did he and Cynthia get along well?'

'Very well,' Hope replied.

Also, there was no testimony at trial to show that Kenny even knew of Candy and Mike's location.

Like everything else that was wrong in Kenny's trial, the very charge of aggravated murder was the wrong charge to be brought against him – even if he was guilty of setting the fire. Aggravated murder is a charge that requires the premeditated intent to kill the person who died. In order to be found guilty of aggravated murder, the prosecution must show that an accused set about to intentionally kill the person. Even the prosecution admitted that no evidence existed that Kenny intended to kill Cynthia. There is a legal principle in Ohio that allows a court to convict a person of murder even though they had intended to murder another person. This is known as 'transferred intent' but it only applies to lesser degrees of murder. It does not apply to capital crimes.

THE VERDICT

The closing arguments for the prosecution and the defence ended the trial. Basinger's monologue, as wordy as his opening statements, included the throwing around of labels like 'psychopath' and 'psychotic killer' among other psychological terms to describe Kenny. He hammered home much of the same claims he made in his opening statement. He did admit some discrepancies in the case and he did admit that Juanita Altimus had her times mixed up about when Kenny made his alleged statements but, as Basinger assured the court, the time when he made the implicating statements wasn't important – the fact that he did make them was what counted.

As for the lack of accelerant traces on Kenny's boots and clothing, Basinger said, 'I want to talk just briefly about the clothes, why there wasn't anything found on these clothes. I mean, he was walking around all night with a drink in his hand and he didn't seem to have any problems doing that – never spilled anything.'

Basinger again impressed upon the three judges that arson definitely caused the fire, saying that he hesitated even to argue the point because he disliked insulting everyone's intelligence. He added that the defence's own consultant agreed with the fire marshal's findings. 'What more needs to be said? And I'm not going to say anything more about that. I can't quite honestly even understand how Mr Kluge can stand up after I'm done and say otherwise. He may.'

Kluge did not argue the arson theory and his failure to do so was the equivalent of committing legal suicide.

The panel of judges adjourned for deliberation then returned to the courtroom less than forty-five minutes later. They dismissed the involuntary manslaughter charge. 'We have, likewise, reached verdicts as it relates to the four remaining counts. At this time, Mr Richey, I am going to ask you to stand please.'

Kenny dropped his head for a second in silent prayer then slowly stood. Still sitting loyally behind him, Steven clasped his hands under his chin, leaning forward on the edge of his seat.

'We, the panel, pursuant to our oaths, find the defendant, Kenneth Richey, guilty of count number one (aggravated murder) . . .'

Kenny's knees buckled and he reached for the support of the table as a cheer resounded from the spectators. They had their lynching.

Kenny only heard the reading of the first count. It mattered little that the court also found him guilty of breaking and entering and child endangerment. His date for sentencing was set for January the twenty-sixth but he didn't hear this either. He only remembers being led from the courtroom in chains, shuffling like a geisha girl. Steven only remembers the glazed look in Kenny's eyes before he wiped tears from his own.

10

SENTENCED TO DEATH

'I'm not certain I can describe how I felt,' Kenny recalls. When he stepped from the courthouse, a few newspaper photographers waited. Kenny faced their cameras and he grinned. 'It was dumb but I didn't think about how this might look. I only wanted to avoid showing them weakness – that I wasn't defeated or affected by what they did to me.'

The resulting photo in the county paper didn't show an unbeaten man. It showed a maniacally grinning, callous man – the embodiment of the kind of character Basinger had portrayed Kenny as throughout the trial. The newspaper article would be framed and placed on the wall of Kluge's office. As he would later explain in an interview with the American documentary, *American Justice*, he kept the picture to serve as a reminder of how bad a job he'd done so he would never again repeat the performance.

Despite Kenny's attempt to show that he was unaffected by the decision, he said, 'I was frustrated, angry – really angry – and confused as to how it could've happened. But mostly, I was traumatised and in shock. When Dad and Steven visited me after the trial, we sat like three mannequins, each of us in our own world. I don't think we said a dozen words between us. Writing to Mum was the hardest thing. I'm only glad she couldn't afford to fly over for the trial because it would've killed her seeing what happened with her own eyes.'

A week after the trial, Kenny attempted suicide. 'When the shock briefly lifted, the fear of living years on death row only to finally be strapped in to the electric chair, gripped me. Why go through all that? I wanted it to end. I wanted the pain to end. So I cut my wrists with a metal ashtray. I was so numb on the outside, I hardly felt any pain, even when a nick on the ashtray's edge snagged my skin and I tugged at it.'

As a result of his suicide attempt on January the sixteenth, that same day, after he was taken to the St Rita's Medical Center in Lima for treatment, deputies transported Kenny to a jail in Lima that was apparently better equipped to handle 'problem prisoners'. When he arrived at the Lima jail, jailers stripped Kenny to his underpants and then handcuffed him to a steel bunk. His wrists were cuffed to the top end of the bunk while his ankles were cuffed to the foot of it. For twenty-four hours, he had no mattress and there was to be no release from the restraints for forty-eight hours. He had to lap food from a tray placed beside him like a dog and drink water through a straw.

On January the twenty-sixth, deputies took him back to Ottawa for sentencing. More serious than first-degree murder, aggravated murder carries one of two mandatory sentences – life imprisonment without the opportunity for parole or death. Which of these two sentences a convicted person receives is determined by balancing the factors involved. If mitigating factors outweigh aggravating factors, leniency will, in theory, be given and a life imprisonment sentence will be imposed. It can, of course, be argued that this is also a death sentence – a long, slow death sentence.

The aggravating factor, the reason for justifying execution in Kenny's case, was that, in the judges' opinion, Kenny had pulled down the smoke detector prior to torching the apartment. This action, the judges stated, belonged to a 'cold, calculating killer'. Of course, no evidence had been presented at trial to prove that

Kenny had pulled the smoke detector down. Even the fire marshal gave a conflicting opinion about this and he did say that 'very intense heat and flame caused [the smoke detector] to melt down'.

As far as mitigating factors were concerned, Kluge relied on the results of several psychological evaluations Kenny had undergone since August 1986 while he awaited trial. Prior to the evaluations, we had exchanged letters on the subject.

I was evaluated several times after my arrest when I faced the probability of trial. The reason for the evaluations was twofold – to establish whether a defence of insanity could be built and to ascertain if there were any mitigating factors should my case go to trial and I was found guilty of aggravated murder. It should be noted that I never pled 'not guilty by reason of insanity' yet the court still granted my psychological evaluations – this serves to confirm again that Kluge erred in making such a plea in Kenny's case.

In the field of law, psychological evaluations are little more than a tool that either the defence or the prosecution in any particular case can use to their benefit. The doctor from my first evaluation concluded that my actions were the result of my LSD use – a 'bad trip'. But this couldn't be used as a defence under Washington law because I had taken the LSD voluntarily. Disappointed with the results of the evaluation, my lawyer implied that I should 'act up' and he gave me pointers about how to do it to the best effect.

In subsequent evaluations, I claimed to be a victim with a background of abuse. I acted emotionless and just sat there stony-faced. When asked to draw pictures as part of the evaluation, I drew objects related to hostility or violence. The result? The shrinks concluded that I suffered from a host of personality disorders which were seen as mitigating factors. Because of this, the State of Washington decided on leniency and withdrew the death penalty in my case.

In theory, America won't execute an insane person. It is the reason so many defence lawyers consider insanity as a defence for their clients in capital murder cases. It is also the reason American courts have set such stringent standards that define what insanity is. For example, an insanity claim will fail if a defendant acknowledges that he knew what he had done was wrong. Crossing the insanity minefield is difficult. Kenny might have made a better go of faking it if he had known he'd have to rely on the results of the evaluations. But they were conducted before his trial, at a time when he didn't believe for a moment he'd be found guilty. I had told Kenny the pointers my attorney had given me and, when he stepped into a bare room in the jail where a doctor sat behind a plain table, he played the game using the tips I'd passed on to him – only he stretched his performance too far. He told a yarn of suffering in a heavily abused background that was full of physical violence. He told how our mum had thrown him out of the house at the age of sixteen and how he'd had to live on the streets for a couple of years, scavenging for food. He told of his uncontrollable mood swings. He said he could see things other people couldn't see and he claimed to hear voices. He couldn't have slapped it on any thicker if he'd used a trowel.

The doctor, William Macintosh, asked Kenny to sketch a picture of a house and he drew a fortress with battlements, parapets, barbed wire and sandbagged walls. From this picture, the doctor concluded that Kenny would have had trouble dealing with the external world. When asked to draw a tree, he sketched a barren dead tree, devoid of leaves and with thorns sticking out of its bark. Analysing this in court, Dr MacIntosh said, 'Well, I see indications that he felt his life had been troubled, that his goals had never been met, that he sees death as an alternative perhaps to go on living because of seeing the tree as something that is dead.' And, when he was asked to draw a person, Kenny delivered a picture of a soldier. Dr

MacIntosh surmised that the soldier gave Kenny a particular sense of identity, adding that it was 'an identity where an individual is seen in an aggressive role'.

Asked to draw a picture of the opposite sex, he produced an open coffin with a stick figure lying in it. 'It's difficult to tell what this meant to me,' Dr MacIntosh said. 'I think I had some problems. I thought, maybe, some guilt was being projected on the part of Mr Richey over past acts. I think, possibly, some of his hostilities and feelings of dissatisfaction with women was also projected into this drawing.'

The doctor asked Kenny for one last drawing. Of this, Dr MacIntosh said, 'I asked him to draw me the scariest thing in the world, the scariest thing he could think of. He, while looking at the blank sheet of paper, remarked to me, "I'm not scared of anything." And I asked him to try to think of something that he was scared of and he did eventually tell me that it could represent water in that he is scared of sharks that might swim in water and attack a person. I think it indicated to me some vague and definite fears that he could not pinpoint where these fears are, such as that you're out on a large ocean. People could come or you could feel attack at anytime. It comes without notice, with the suddenness of a shark attack.'

Kenny's creative performance did not go unnoticed. At the sentencing hearing, Basinger asked another doctor, Leena Puhakka, 'Wouldn't you agree that, throughout all of this [evaluation], the defendant was attempting to manipulate and feed you information, attempting to control the outcome? Isn't that a fair assumption?'

'Yes,' Dr Puhakka said.

A Dr Antoine Demosthene also saw through the facade, saying that she quickly came up with a diagnosis that Kenny suffered from an anti-social personality 'because eighty to ninety percent of his information, although we had a great relationship throughout the evaluation, was completely false.'

They dubbed Kenny a 'manipulator' and, because of this, he had a 'personality disorder'. Dr Puhakka stated that Kenny had an emotional mentality of a two-year-old while Dr Demosthene concluded that Kenny had the emotional mentality of a fifteen- to eighteen-year-old.

In an attempt to guarantee no leniency was shown by the judges, Basinger tried to provoke Dad. Shortly after Steven and Dad entered the courtroom for the sentencing hearing, Kluge approached and told Dad that Basinger wanted to talk. Kluge said that someone claiming to be 'Kenny's brother' attempted to visit Kenny at the Lima jail.

'No way,' Dad replied, adding that Steven had been with him all day.

Kluge led my dad into an office where Prosecutor Gershultz sat behind a desk. Basinger stood behind Gershultz. Kluge then left the office, leaving Dad with the two of them. Mentioning nothing about any attempted visit at the Lima jail, Basinger spewed a tirade, attacking me, not Kenny, by using names like 'monster' and 'animal'. Dad kept his cool and replied, 'The boy who shot those people isn't the son I know.'

Basinger ignored him and continued his tirade and accused Dad of raising me wrongly. Next, he turned to Kenny, accusing Dad of raising another murderer. Then he struck out at Steven and asked when they could expect him to murder someone. The urge to pummel Basinger tugged at Dad but he resisted it and turned and walked from the office. He saw it for what it was – a set up. Had he gone for Basinger, the assault would've been brought out at the sentencing hearing and used to support Basinger's claim that the Richeys are a violent family and any consideration for leniency would've been jeopardised.

Later, Dad suspected that Kluge had known that Gershultz and Basinger had no intention of discussing any alleged attempted jail visit. It was a lure to bait him to come into the office. Dad would forever believe that Kluge and the prosecution had been in collusion from the beginning. It should be said, however, that neither Kluge nor the prosecution ever admitted collusion and, despite Dad's suspicions, there was no direct evidence to suggest that such a conclusion could be drawn. It's certainly possible that Kluge could just as easily have been duped by the alleged jail visit information.

Following the testimony of the shrinks and that of our dad, the judges took a short recess. They returned minutes later to a still courtroom. The presiding judge, Michael J. Corrigan, said, 'The panel of three judges has considered and weighed against the aggravating circumstances that Kenny Richey was convicted beyond a reasonable doubt, the nature and circumstances of the offence, the history, character and background of Kenneth Richey and all the factors enumerated in the Ohio Revised Code. The panel of three judges unanimously finds, beyond a reasonable doubt, that the aggravating circumstances Kenny Richey was found guilty of committing outweigh any mitigating factors opposed to it. That having been found, Mr Richey, would you please stand?'

Kenny got to his feet, numbed, aware that the sentence they would pass would be death.

'Is there anything, sir, you want to say before the court imposes sentence?' Corrigan said.

Kenny knew there was nothing he could say to alter their decision. He rolled his eyes. 'Not really. You found me guilty of a crime I didn't commit. Go ahead.'

Corrigan nodded. 'As it relates to count one, based upon the findings of the court, you will be sentenced to die in the electric chair on June thirtieth, nineteen-eighty-seven, at six o'clock in the morning. That is the anniversary date of Cynthia Collins' death. You will be transported from Putnam County to the Chillicothe Correctional Institution, I believe, and will subsequently be transported and will stay on death row until such time as you are executed.'

'You've made a big mistake,' Kenny mumbled. 'You've made a fucking big mistake.'

11

DEATH ROW

After three hours of being processed at the Chilicothe Correctional Institution, Kenny was transferred in chains and with an armed escort to the Southern Ohio Correctional Facility (about a two hours' drive from Columbus Grove). His appeal, filed automatically, postponed his execution date and it would take the Ohio Court of Appeals two and a half years to render a decision on the appeal.

Kenny found a bundle of bedding on the bare, fluid-stained mattress of cell K4-14, his new home. His short hair had dried in an uncombed spike from the shower all new arrivals are subjected to. It came after the customary strip-search and the order to bend over and expose his anus. After the shower, under the vigilant gaze of several guards, he dressed, pulling on trousers that had a thin blood-red stripe running the length of each leg. 'Dead man's stripes,' a guard eagerly told him.

The cell was a cramped space, barely wider than his outstretched arms. It was similar to his county jail cell with a steel desk bolted to the wall at the end of the steel bunk. Scores of initials were scraped and etched into the cream-colored surface of the table and he wondered how many of these men had met their fate in the electric chair. In front of the desk was a steel stool embedded into the concrete like a giant thumbtack. Against the rear wall of the cell, a steel toilet and sink stood, above

145

which a thin chromium layered mirror produced a distorted reflection due to the number of knuckle dents that had been pounded into its surface – spending twenty-three hours a day inside the cramped cell, Kenny would soon come to understand this means of prisoners venting their frustration.

He lowered himself to the bare mattress and dropped his head. He stared at his plimsoll shoes. An assortment of rock, country and western, blues, rap and even classical played from over two dozen radios in other cells. Daytime talk-show hosts quizzed their guests, an audience clapped, a woman screamed, gunshots . . . all tinny television sounds. Blacks yelled at one another in their bastard ghetto tongues, saying little of substance. A steel barred door rolled and clanged shut, its reverberation resonating along the twenty-cell double-decker tier. The stench of shit drifted under his nose and a toilet flushed. What sunlight there was penetrating the thick windows along the outer wall of the cellblock illuminated cigarette smoke that hung along the tier like a battleground haze.

This was death row. This would be his life until he won his appeal or until they walked him to the electric chair. Edinburgh was a distant place of distant memories. It felt to him as if he lived in Britain a lifetime ago. A nightmare had become reality. The pressure squeezed slowly at first but then he could feel it from all sides and it was closing in. It felt as if he couldn't breathe. He felt helpless. Everything flashed through his mind – his limbs cuffed and chained, the dehumanising strip-searches, the courtroom faces, the liars' faces, the verdict, the cheering spectators, the passing of sentence . . .

He released a long-confined growl and leapt from the bunk. A wooden footlocker sat against the wall of the cell. He grabbed it and lifted it above his shoulders and he brought it down upon the steel toilet again and again, until the wood splintered and littered the cell. Then he collapsed to the cool concrete, placed his head in his hands and cried.

The tier had quietened. Then a television sounded and another, then music, talking and someone yelling, 'Welcome to the row!' Laughter.

Welcome to the row. A hammer pounded his head, behind his left eye – it was to be the first of many regular migraines he'd suffer through the years. He crawled on to the mattress, not caring about the stains, wrapped himself in a ball of self-pity and closed his eyes, trying to shut everything out, wishing he could escape the madness.

A guard woke him some time later to thrust a plastic food tray through the hatch of the cell bars. The guard questioned him about the smashed locker. Kenny shrugged. Ten minutes after the guard disappeared, a 'goon squad', consisting of five guards wearing space age storm-trooper suits, rushed into his cell and cuffed him. They escorted him to segregation. He served three days in 'the hole'. In addition to this punishment, they charged him for destruction of State property and the prison infirmary prescribed him the antidepressant Thorozine, a drug that suppresses aggression. For two months, he walked the 'Thorozine shuffle'. They needn't have bothered because he didn't explode again. Years later, the prison warden dubbed him a 'model prisoner'.

On the morning of February the tenth 1987, two weeks after the paddy wagon had raced Kenny to prison, a woman, Karen Punches, telephoned Dad. Mrs Punches and her husband ran the Lee Bell Motel in Ottawa, where Fire Marshal Cryer had rented a room. She told Dad that she had asked Cryer about the fire at the Old Farm Village Apartment Complex and about the rumoured negative forensic lab results from Kenny's clothing. Cryer admitted to Mrs Punches that they had found nothing either way to convict Kenny or clear him.

Some days later, following Kenny's conviction, Mrs Punches asked Cryer what convicted Kenny of the crime. Pointing to his mouth, Cryer stated, 'His mouth.' Kenny had never made any incriminating statements so it has to be assumed that Cryer was referring to Kenny's frequent threats against Basinger and Cryer.

Mrs Punches also informed Dad that, on January the fourth, Bob Dannenger checked into the motel. Mrs Punches was instructed to send his bill to Basinger – Basinger had called Dannenberg to testify as a witness.

In Mrs Punches words, 'When Mr Dannenberg came into the office that evening, we started talking about the little girl that died in the fire and he said he was told that she was raped and that he didn't really want to leave his home out of State and work (*sic*), but he was here for the sake of the little girl, on her behalf, because she was raped.'

How many other witnesses did Basinger tell this fallacy to? It could explain the lies and inconsistencies spewed by witnesses over the courtroom. What witness, if they'd been led to believe that Cynthia had been raped before tragically dying in that fire, wouldn't embellish the truth in order to help convict a person they believed was a child molester?

Mrs Punches believed Kenny had been made into a scapegoat and she advised Dad to investigate the case. Since Kenny's sentencing on January the twenty-sixth, Dad had been living like a Londoner during World War II. He'd been bunkered in his apartment, hoping to survive the bombs that had been blowing his family apart. Mrs Punches hadn't been the only person to suggest that he investigate the case. Others made remarks suggesting that the trial had been a public lynching. Dad had been prohibited from attending the trial because he'd been listed as a witness although, in the end, he wasn't called to give evidence.

Karen Punches had been the first person to contact Dad to offer to provide an affidavit to what she had witnessed. When he learned that Merrian Blye never testified, Dad contacted her. It was at this point he discovered that Kluge failed even to interview the woman. Dad went to see Mrs Blye and obtained her affidavit too.

About eight months after trial, Kenny received a cardboard box that contained legal documents relating to his case. In the box, he found a list with potential witnesses for the defence. Among the names on the list were three people who were never called to the stand – Hope's ex-husband, Robert Collins, Fire Chief Len Hefner and Merrian Blye. All three were people who, had they taken the stand, could have contradicted the prosecution's case. Why did Kluge fail to call these witnesses?

As well as Karen Punches and Merrian Blye, Dad wanted to question others, particularly those who attended the party, but, strangely, they had all moved – it was as if they were running away from something. However, a breakthrough came with Peggy Price. With her conscience apparently eating at her, she penned Kenny a letter and confided a few things. Peggy admitted knowing of three occasions on which Cynthia had started or attempted to start fires in Hope's apartment. She also admitted that Hope was in the habit of pulling the smoke alarm from its ceiling mount to disconnect it whenever they had parties or when they smoked pot.

Dad quickly got Peggy to agree to an affidavit and she gave it on April the sixteenth 1987. However, it was to be the last affidavit obtained until May 1992 – a few months after Kenny's case had come to public attention in Britain.

During those five years of anonymity, Kenny had slid farther into a dark pit of depression and he sat at the bottom of this pit, helpless. Initially, he had repeatedly told prison staff and the death row counsellor that he was innocent but he grew frustrated by their rolling eyes and sceptical comments. Some of the guards even treated him worse as a result of his claims. He learned to keep his mouth shut, to go with the programme. He'd been convicted after a trial and, as far as they were concerned, he was guilty and awaiting execution – he had nothing else to offer the world. The last thing they wanted to hear was another snivelling prisoner proclaiming his innocence.

149

It insulted a system they wholeheartedly believed was fair and just.

Yet, for our parents, life was nearly as difficult as Kenny's. They had one son on death row and another serving sixty-five years in prison. Mum bottled her pain up inside. She tried to pretend life was normal and she kept our circumstances a secret from her friends and relatives. She kept up the pretence that her boys were still serving in the military – relatives were unaware of Kenny's earlier discharge and his divorce. We had all agreed that the charade would spare her endless questions and embarrassment. For years, she carried her secret burden. 'The worst part was when I went home after work and closed the door on life – that was when I was hit with the reality of it all,' she said. When the reality became public knowledge, the reaction from most people was supportive.

Feeling unwelcome at the Old Farm Village Apartment Complex, Dad moved to a house in Ottawa in the closing months of 1988. He lived there with Steven for a year until an opportunity to manage an antique store lured him to Washington State and Steven soon followed, accompanied by his girlfriend, Kelly. Our dad had visited Kenny before leaving Ohio and he visited me when he passed through the dusty town of Walla Walla, Washington. The town is famous for only two things – sweet onions and the State penitentiary. When I asked Dad how Kenny had seemed, he described him as being bitter.

Heavily in debt, the antique business my dad took over collapsed within weeks. But, there was some good to come out of a bad situation. Through the business, he met a woman, Lee, and, within six months, they got married. Steven and Kelly returned to Ohio. Ironically, they found a vacant flat in the Old Farm Village Apartment Complex. My dad and Lee travelled back to Ohio and bought a home in the rural town of Kalida, about a dozen miles from Columbus Grove.

For them, life went on but, for Kenny, life became his appeals. They were all that mattered. Yet, he knew the odds. A man condemned to die in America is usually executed or he spends the remainder of his life behind bars. Under one percent of death row inmates ever see freedom again. The light at the end of his long tunnel appeared faint. Yet, some things, such as the affidavits our dad had collected, gave him hope. Also, among his legal papers that he received eight months after his trial, he discovered a statement made by a Dr Thomas Dicke of the St Rita's Lima Medical Center in Lima, where Cynthia's body had been taken. Dr Dicke stated that, after Hope entered the medical centre, she made the remark that Cynthia may have started the fire because she had started fires before. It supported Peggy Price's affidavit.

In 1989, Kenny finally received a decision from the Ohio Court of Appeals (the first court in an extensive appellate process). They upheld the trial court's decision. It was the first of the many disappointments that would follow. However, he had expected the rejection – he'd learned from other death row inmates that the Court of Appeals always leaves major decisions on capital punishment cases for the higher appellate courts and this is particularly true in cases that have been decided by a panel of judges rather than by a jury of citizens. The two and a half years he'd served on death row had been dead time – a waste.

As our dad said, Kenny had indeed become bitter. Hatred for the American judicial system festered in him. He felt his youth had been stolen and, even if he won an appeal, how long would it take? It had already taken two and a half years for a decision whose outcome had always been predictable. Other prisoners gave him some solace. Several of them, who had used their time inside to become knowledgeable about the law, read his trial transcripts and, although they offered different opinions on Kenny's case, they all agreed on two things – he hadn't received a fair trial and they doubted he was guilty. Yet, he knew it didn't matter what they thought – only the appellate court's opinion mattered and he wasn't holding his breath for that.

Kenny had been warned by prisoners who had gone through the State appellate process that he shouldn't harbour high expectations of the State Supreme Court. Rarely, if ever, did this court overrule a decision of State judges. It concerned Kenny. His new lawyer, Jane Perry, from the Ohio State Public Defenders Office, prepared an appeal to the Ohio Supreme Court. He had little confidence in her and this was not solely because of his experience with Kluge. The Public Defender's Office was understaffed and overworked and, given the failure of death row appeals, he questioned her dedication. He knew he needed a polished lawyer but that would require thousands of dollars – money our family just didn't have.

Kenny had no choice but to accept and play the cards he had been dealt and hope, by some miracle, Jane Perry would rise to the occasion. He also knew that he had to adjust to the idea that the Ohio Supreme Court would take at least two years before rendering their decision on his appeal.

He had already served two years on death row and he had managed to adapt to his environment. He had made some friends and sometimes they kicked a ball around or played cards for one hour a day. Although Kenny and the rest of the death row prisoners were segregated from the general population of prisoners, they did share the same recreation rights. This was limited to an hour, which would be spent either outside in a tennis-court-sized yard surrounded by a high wall or inside in a small gym. The remainder of Kenny's time, other than ten minutes for a shower, was spent alone in his cell. There were two death row tiers, each holding forty men, but another tier would be added in 1992 to house the increased number of condemned men. Each tier used the yard separately so Kenny only got to know the men on his own tier.

Exercise equipment was limited to parallel dip bars but few used the bars. The most telling difference between prisoners in general population and death row prisoners is physical. Generally, prisoners are in a healthy condition but those on death row often carry a paunch, their muscle tone smoothed by inactivity. Why bother exercising? Bigger muscles won't prevent the inevitable – the electric chair does not discriminate.

The threat of death Kenny assured me, does hang like a cloud above death row. Most of the prisoners made jokes of it, as if in defiance, but probably more from a state of denial – the mind's defence. Kenny's own attitude varied depending on his mood or depending on how frequent his nightmares were. He described them, saying, 'I've been having the nightmares since shortly after arriving on death row. It's a similar nightmare every time. Sometimes Basinger is throwing the switch of the electric chair or sometimes the witnesses in the spectators' room are cheering as the switch is thrown. Other times, there's no one watching. It's a graphic nightmare. I remember every detail of it. It always wakes me just as the switch is thrown. I wonder what those shrinks would've made of it? Hey, maybe you can call your book, *Does the Nightmare Ever End* or *Nightmare on Death Row* – or how about *To Fry or Not to Fry* or *Fry, Fry and Fry Again*.'

His nightmares, it seems, revealed that, behind his facade, the prospect of execution tormented him more than he let on. At least he managed to retain his sense of humour, morbid though it may be.

Kenny passed much of his time writing letters, writing poetry, reading and watching the twelve-inch black-and-white television in his cell – his porthole to the world. His poetry was sometimes enlightening:

> Silence prevails in this dark lonely world,
> As my voice cries out alone and unheard.

Reaching out, I grasp nothing but air,
Searching the darkness, finding only despair.
How long must I suffer this torment and pain?
With each passing day, I feel I'm going insane.
Solitary confinement to a small concrete cell,
This dark lonely world has become my private hell.
In this nightmare I am forced to reside,
While, little by little, I feel myself dying inside.

As the years passed following Kenny's conviction, we maintained regular correspondence. He kept me updated regarding the affidavits and other discoveries of his case but I did little more than shake my head in disbelief that he had ever been convicted and I placed the information on a shelf in my mind. We lived in separate – though similar – worlds two thousand miles apart and I couldn't see how I could do anything for him other than provide words of support. Yet, guilt periodically tugged at me. I felt partly responsible for Kenny's ordeal and I felt that I should do more to help – I just couldn't figure out how.

In 1991, I read an article in a magazine about an innocent man who had been released from death row in Texas but it had taken twelve years of trying to prove his innocence before freedom opened its arms to him. Twelve years! And the man would have been in prison longer – or even executed – had his case not received public attention. It was through this attention that a good lawyer became interested in his case and agreed to represent him. It also led to the court being less dismissive of his appeal. It was then that I realised I did have what was needed to help Kenny – an abundance of time. Time to read up on his case, time to understand the errors made in it and time to write about them.

I told Kenny of my idea and asked him to send all of his trial documents and transcripts. It wasn't easy. I had to do battle with the Washington prison administration to allow me to have Kenny's legal work and then I had to do battle with the distractions of prison life, such as the noise and the frequent cell searches that would leave my notes and papers in disarray. Studying his case became my focus for several months.

As August 1991, approached, Kenny wrote of two things – his appeal (Oral Arguments) hearing before the Ohio Supreme Court and seeing our mum. She planned to fly to America for a couple of weeks. However, because the cost of travelling from Ohio to Washington State was almost as much as the cost of flying to the States from the UK, she would be unable to visit me. But I was satisfied with being able to make lengthy phone calls while she stayed with Steven and Kelly.

Of the anticipated visit, Kenny wrote, 'Well, just seventeen more days until Mum arrives. I'm looking forward to it. I miss her. I only wish they'd let me hug her. One of my greatest fears is Mum dying while I'm still in this place. I have so much to make up to Mum and Dad and I want the chance to do that.' Kenny went on to admit carrying guilt for being in the position to allow Putnam County authorities to frame him. 'I should never have stayed so long in that apartment complex, wasting my life. One thing I've learned after being on death row is that life, no matter how bad it can seem out there, can get worse. I swear, if I never see the inside of a prison cell again, it will still be too soon.'

After his mid August visit from our mum, he wrote, 'Man, it was brilliant seeing Mum again. I missed giving her a hug though. You'd think the bastards would've allowed us at least that because of the distance she travelled and the length of time we haven't seen each other. It's my mother for Christsakes . . . It was really great – my head is still in the clouds. I only wish you could've gotten to see her.'

Their visit took place in a booth and they were divided by a sheet of bullet-resistant glass. They had to communicate through a metal grill. 'That was a humiliating, heartbreaking experience,' Mum said of the non-contact visit. Even the attitude of the guards offended her. They acted as if they resented having to waste their time accommodating the visit. 'Why did they have to be so callous?' she wondered.

Uplifted by the visit from our mum, Kenny turned his mind to the Oral Arguments scheduled for October. The court wouldn't permit Kenny to attend the Oral Arguments hearing so, without his presence in the courtroom, Jane Perry would have just thirty minutes to convince the seven Ohio Supreme Court judges that Kenny deserved his conviction to be over-turned or, at the very least, a new trial. Kenny believed his chances of receiving a fair decision rested on the possibility of drawing public attention to the case. Only then, maybe, would public pressure force the judges to pay closer attention to his case. He wrote to several US prisoner support organisations but his pleas were largely ignored.

Dad did as much as he believed he could. He wrote extensively to the American press and TV but, like Kenny's efforts, his attempts to increase awareness of Kenny's case also met brick walls. Nobody in America seemed to care. I believe it was an attitude born out of ignorance and forged by the persuasiveness of the American media. When I arrived in America, it was communism and the Soviet Union that the media used to stir up paranoia in the masses. When the Berlin Wall collapsed, the media turned its focus on crime as the new enemy that threatened the infrastructure of the American way of life. In the early nineties, they were fighting their so-called 'War on Drugs' and enforcing mandatory exceptional sentences and, if politicians failed to voice their campaign promise of 'Hard Time for Crime', their chances of being elected were slim. The American law enforcement community and its legal system became a juggernaut barrelling through America, convicting and executing people at an alarming rate. Kenny's case was simply a bump in the roadway and the drivers of that judicial juggernaut, the judges, did not want to stop and investigate the damage that had been done. To do so would affect the momentum of their juggernaut. To do so would distort the image of a system that the American public believed to be so righteous and infallible. Kenny was just another guilty, desperate scumbag pleading innocence.

I referred Kenny to the London-based support group, Prisoners Abroad, an established charitable organisation that helps British citizens imprisoned overseas. However, he was to discover that all he could expect from them was a letter to the court on his behalf. The problem, as Prisoners Abroad had found out when they looked into his case, lay in Kenny's citizenship. Officially, he was an American national. This information shocked Kenny. Although born in Zeist in Holland, from the time he was a toddler until he was eighteen, he'd lived in Edinburgh – he'd been educated there, had worked there, had paid taxes there . . . his heart was there. Despite travelling to America under a US passport, he believed he held a dual nationality as Steven and I do.

As a result of this information, he attempted to file an application for UK citizenship but he received no response. The British Foreign Office abstained from even commenting on his situation. They did, however, inform our mum that a person could only obtain British citizenship after living in the UK for five or more years and by applying for citizenship while residing in the UK. This battle for his citizenship would not be resolved for many years.

Having been unsuccessful in drawing attention to his case, Kenny was relieved to learn that his Oral Arguments were postponed until March the seventeenth 1992. It gave him more time to try to highlight his case. But, by January 1992, desperation screamed from his letters. 'It feels like Lady Luck is against me because I can't seem to catch a break. No one listens, Tom. Sometimes it feels like there's a huge conspiracy to keep me down.'

By then, I had combed through his case and I was convinced of his innocence. I was ready to help yet, given the rejection Dad received from the US media, I suspected I could pound on their front door as much as I liked and they'd never open it. I figured the only way to get Kenny's story out there was by trying to interest the British press in it. If they became involved, the US press might reconsider and look at the story. So I set about writing a summary of Kenny's case, pointing out its flaws and questioning his conviction. I had a friend in Edinburgh send me *The Writer's Handbook*, which lists the addresses of nearly every publisher in the UK, and I started from there. In late February 1992, I picked a handful of newspapers and sent a letter and a summary of Kenny's case to each of them. I also wrote to Mum, warning her that our dirty linen might soon be flapping in the wind for all to see.

A few days into March, the prison's Public Information Officer stopped by my cell. She told me a reporter from the *News of the World* had phoned the prison and requested an interview with me. I agreed. The reporter arrived a day or two later and I was taken to the visiting area. However, only a few minutes into the interview, I realised it was a mistake. The reporter, a Liverpudlian living in New York, stepped into the non-contact visiting booth, said, 'Hi!' and then launched into an endless stream of questions. I'd seen his kind of face before – the same needy face the jail's drug addicts wore when the prison was dry.

Most of his questions sought answers of pure sensationalism. He asked things like 'Have you ever experienced sexual harassment from other prisoners?' – a question completely unrelated to Kenny's case.

When I said, 'No', he pressed the matter.

'Look,' I said, 'you've been watching too many prison films.'

When he continued to ask questions about me rather than about Kenny's case, I ended the interview, feeling totally used.

Fortunately, that same week, a letter from *The Mail on Sunday* arrived, saying that the editor was interested in learning more about Kenny's case. I sent a more detailed letter to one of their reporters in Ohio, who faxed it to London. On March the thirteenth, a reporter from *The Mail on Sunday* appeared at the Washington Corrections Center to interview me. Although cautious due to my experience with the tabloid reporter, I agreed to the interview.

As soon as I stepped into the visiting booth, the reporter erased all my concerns when he displayed sympathy and sincerity for Kenny. I knew he represented the kind of paper that would take Kenny's case seriously.

12

DID KENNY KILL?

On March the fifteenth, two days before Kenny's Oral Arguments, the centre spread of *The Mail on Sunday* carried a picture of Kenny's face as a teenager, a recent gloomy-faced photo of Mum holding framed photos of Kenny and me (reporters had been to interview her too) and one of me that had been snapped during the interview a few days before. The headline read, 'TWO THOUSAND MILES APART. TWO MURDERS. TOM FACES SIXTY-FIVE YEARS. KENNY FACES THE ELECTRIC CHAIR. BUT DID KENNY KILL?' The accompanying article cited a couple of glaring points over the mishandling of the evidence in Kenny's case.

It was the rolling boulder that caused an avalanche of media attention from other national and local UK papers. *The Scotsman* printed an article a couple of days later, detailing more facts about his case and they also printed a letter from Kenny. It read, in part:

> I am fighting for a new trial, which is all I want. I do not seek, nor do I want, a pardon as a pardon is for someone being forgiven for a crime they have committed. I have committed no crime . . . I only seek a new trial.

As far as I'm aware, only the *Daily Express* printed a negative article. If I remember correctly, its headline read, 'BABYKILLER SEEKS MERCY'. I tore it up in disgust. But, within a couple of weeks, they reversed their negative stance as further facts supporting Kenny's innocence appeared in the quality press.

In Ohio, on March the seventeenth, Jane Perry argued in the State Supreme Court for the new trial that Kenny sought. Prohibited from introducing new evidence at this stage of the appeal process, she raised three issues: the lack of sufficient evidence to convict Kenny; the contamination of evidence through police mishandling it; and the prejudicial threats Kenny had made against the prosecutor.

In a letter to me, Ms Perry wrote, 'I was prepared to argue other issues but did not get to them. The judges asked a lot of questions on both sides. I am not, however, overly optimistic that the judges will order a new trial. We have a very conservative court here and they are most reluctant to overturn a conviction, particularly when the trial has been held before a panel of judges as it was in your brother's case.'

The attitude of the Ohio Supreme Court could be summed up in the line of questioning that ended with a Freudian slip. The court asked Ms Perry, 'Isn't it fair to say that the evidence against the defendant is overwhelming?'

Ms Perry replied, 'I do not agree that the evidence of guilt in this case is overwhelming. It is a circumstantial evidence case. There is no scientific physical evidence that connects Kenny Richey to this fire. In fact, his clothing and the boots he was wearing were sent to a laboratory for testing and came back negative for the presence of accelerants, that is the materials that were used to start the fire.'

The Court asked, 'For the presence of what?'

Ms Perry answered, 'Accelerants – materials that are used to start arson fires or any fires for that matter.'

The Court queried, 'Well, he used kerosene, didn't he? Not he – but somebody did?'

If this last remark is not indicative of prejudgement and blind support for the prosecution, I don't know what is.

Despite the court's obvious bias, it would take months for them to consider and render an opinion regarding Kenny's case. Putting caution aside, Kenny began to feel optimism grow inside him. He just couldn't see how the court could ignore the fact that they had an innocent man on death row, particularly when the British media had taken an interest. Like frenzied sharks, they tore into the story, inundating the court, Kenny's prison and the Ohio Public Defenders Office with calls. It took two months before the first American newspaper reported the story.

Jane Perry couldn't handle the British media. 'This is pack journalism like I've never seen it,' she said and, before the end of March, she refused to talk to any British press (though she later had no problem talking with an American reporter for an American newspaper). She reasoned that the media attention was 'bad' for Kenny's case but she didn't explain why she believed this.

As a result of the media blitzkrieg on the Southern Ohio Correctional Facility, the warden placed a media ban on Kenny. Until November the first 1992, no interviews with him were permitted. Before the ban was implemented, he did do two interviews. A reporter for *The Mail on Sunday* interviewed him the day after his Oral Arguments and *BBC Scotland* conducted an interview over the phone with him.

The Mail on Sunday printed a second article following Kenny's interview. Titled 'LIVING HELL OF DEATH ROW BRITON', it pictured Kenny, handcuffed, standing beside a guard. It was the first time I'd seen him since 1985. He looked the same as I remembered, except for his eyes. His eyes reminded me of the hollow sockets of desperation I'd seen on old newsreels of concentration camp victims.

The article began:

'It's a living hell,' says Kenny in his soft Edinburgh burr. He is slouched forward in his chair, his hands shackled before him . . . 'It's the noise of the day I can't stand. I suffer migraines so I stuff wet toilet paper in my ears and wrap a towel around my head. That keeps out the worst of it. And I sleep through the day. At night, I read my mail, if I've got any. I like to get letters, that's what keeps me going. I live for the silence of the night. That's when I think about what's important. Home is on my mind. I work out in detail just what I'm going to do when I go back. I relive the things I did when I was there.

'When it comes to the death sentence, I feel angry, cheated. I think about it sometimes but most of the time I try to shove it away. I only ask for one thing in the end. I want my body to go back to Scotland because it's terrible to think of America as my final resting place.'

The article showed his contradictory patterns of thought – his hope and belief that he will return home one day but also the acknowledgment that, in the end, his appeals may fail and he'll be executed.

Following British media attention, stacks of mail offering support, concern and a few kind words arrived daily for Kenny. In two weeks, the letters passed the one-hundred-and-fifty mark. He even received a letter from the Archbishop of Cincinnati, Ohio, who had been contacted by the Archbishop of Saint Andrew's, Edinburgh, asking that Kenny be given church help in his appeal. The Archbishop of Canterbury also became involved. The British government, however, were silent.

And that is how he lived his days. He vacillated between thoughts of life and death. Kenny once wrote:

It's a unique situation to be in. This conglomerate of people have taken everything from me, including the unseen things like pride and dignity, and they have absolute control over me. They alone determine when and where and at what time I'll die.

I'd be lying if I denied ever considering suicide. Sometimes the pain and helplessness becomes so unbearable, suicide seems like a painless solution. But I think about Mum and Dad and how painful it is for them too. And I think about those weasels, Basinger and Cryer. If I committed suicide, they'd win, wouldn't they? I can't let that happen. I didn't start the fire and I didn't kill that child and it's become important to me to see this through and clear my name.

He found little things to uplift him. Mail would arrive and raise his spirits and he would see light at the end of the tunnel but, inevitably, his spirits would sink again and the light at the end of the tunnel was coming from the beckoning execution chamber. Death row was a continuous emotional struggle.

In April, *This Week*, a Thames Television news programme, contacted our family to express interest in airing a programme about Kenny's case. But, when the producers discovered that the media ban on Kenny remained firm, they hesitated. It became a big issue for Kenny. He believed that exposure of his case on such a nationally respected programme would bolster his claim that he was innocent – provided, of course, that the programme's investigators sided with him rather than the State.

Their decision whether to film or not was affected by another article in *The Mail on Sunday*. 'I AM A REPORTER, NOT A DETECTIVE, BUT I SAY THIS MAN WAITING ON DEATH ROW IS INNOCENT' was the headline. Supporting the points detailed in my letter to them, the article convinced many people of the flaws in his case.

A day after the article, Alistair Darling MP contacted Mum and offered to help. He was the first British politician to become involved. He began by writing the US ambassador first, urging him to use his influence to grant Kenny a reprieve. However, upon learning that Kenny's appeal process had not yet been exhausted and that time for a final reprieve had not yet arrived, Darling turned his efforts elsewhere, focusing particularly on the British Foreign Office. He intended to try to persuade them to step in should the court uphold Kenny's conviction.

'When a Briton is facing the death penalty in a third world country, there is Foreign Office outcry and even pleas from the Queen. Yet the silence in this case has been deafening. It seems nobody wants to offend the Americans,' MP Darling was quoted as saying by a *Guardian* reporter.

In a letter to the editor of *The Scotsman*, Kenny too expressed his frustration.

> The British government is using any device available to avoid getting involved and weasel out of its responsibilities for fear of offending the United States. I have worked and paid taxes as a British citizen. I have a British National Insurance Number. I was treated as a British citizen for nearly eighteen years and I grew up and lived in Scotland. For all intents and purposes, I am a British citizen.

The month of May 1992 saw Alistair Darling's efforts bear fruit. The Foreign Office responded in writing, stating that, if Kenny's appeal was unsuccessful, they would consider an informal plea for clemency.

And that month brought more news, this time in Ohio. A reporter for *The Mail on Sunday* found and interviewed Hope Collins who had remarried. Hope had adopted her new husband's name of Sterling and had given birth again. At this time, the child was five years old. During the interview, Hope admitted calling the fire department *twice* in the ten days preceding the fire at her Columbus Grove apartment because smoke would suddenly gather near the kitchen and living-room ceilings – on the stand, she had testified that this happened between three and six weeks before the fire. She also told the reporter, 'Kenny was always honest and he was always decent. He loved kids. I can't picture him hurting any child. I don't want him to die.'

Days later, the first and only significant article in the American press to raise questions about Kenny's guilt appeared in the newspaper, *The Toledo Blade*. As a result of this, Dad received a phone call from Mrs Sandra Garret. She was the first tenant to live in Hope's apartment after the fire. My dad followed up on Mrs Garret's information by getting her to agree to give an affidavit. Mrs Garret swore that 'on or around June 1989, Pattie Miree (Juanita Altimus's daughter) and myself were discussing the fire that occurred at the apartment in which Kenny Richey had been convicted of. Pattie Miree made the statement to me that her mother lied when she testified at the trial of Kenny Richey.' She also swore that 'Pattie said Kenny was hysterical and tried to get to the child he believed to be in the burning apartment. Pattie also said she did not believe Kenny Richey could have set the fire.'

And something else also happened in May. British fire investigator, Andrew Terry, and solicitor, Andrew McCooey, flew to America and they called on Dad. They represented Freedom Now, a British organisation that assists or represents wrongly convicted Britons in foreign countries. They preferred to work discreetly and had successfully avoided publicity despite their one hundred per cent track record in freeing Britons in Greece, Spain, France and the USA. Their purpose in Ohio? To quietly investigate Kenny's case. They tried to talk to Kenny while in Ohio but the prison warden denied them visitation.

After they concluded their investigation, they invited Dad to dinner. Over the dinner table, they told him that they were convinced that Kluge had been in collusion with the prosecution but they could not agree to take on the case just yet – they had to evaluate all the information they had collected and they needed to read Kenny's court transcripts. They said they would be in touch.

As May stepped aside for the month of June, a crew from *This Week* arrived in the United States to begin filming. Also, in this same month, Lothians MEP, David Martin, called for the United States to retry Kenny. Martin told the European Parliament there were serious doubts over the safety of Kenny's conviction.

June delivered more developments. During filming, the crew of *This Week* visited the Putnam County landfill where, within five minutes, they coincidentally saw petrol and paint thinner cans lying on top of piles of rubbish. More importantly, the programme's reporter, Debbie Davies, interviewed many of the key figures involved. She spoke to Prosecutor Gershultz, who reaffirmed his claim that 'everything was done correctly and above board'.

It was Ms Davies who discovered the previously unknown information about the carpet having been unrolled in front of the petrol pumps in the parking lot. Steve Stechschulte, now a candidate for the post of police chief, admitted, 'It was a mistake to unroll the carpet in front of the gasoline pumps on the forecourt.'

Other additional information also came to light. Although Juanita Altimus still maintained that Kenny had made a remark when the smoking chair was thrown from Hope's burnt apartment, she told Debbie Davies she had said she may have misheard exactly what he said because of his accent. She stated Kenny may have said, 'The firemen did a hell of a job, didn't they?' instead of her prior testimony that Kenny remarked, 'I did a hell of a job, didn't I?'

And Juanita's daughter, Pattie Miree, told Debbie, 'She (Juanita) gets things twisted and mixed up when she's excited.'

Peggy Price was also interviewed and she said, 'Hope definitely disconnected the smoke detector.' Peggy claimed she was certain of this because she remembered that Hope pulled down the smoke detector early in the evening of the party after they cooked pork chops which had caused the apartment to fill with smoke.

When Debbie Davies questioned Hope about pulling down the smoke detector on the night of the party, she admitted, 'I can't remember but it's possible I disconnected it.'

Of course, the reason the three judges sentenced Kenny to death was because they believed he pulled down the smoke detector.

This Week also tried to interview Kenny's lawyer, Jane Perry, but she claimed she was too busy. This infuriated Kenny and he told me Ms Perry's days as his lawyer were numbered. She seemed to be taking little interest to his case, he said. For example, she had neglected to take an affidavit from the apartment complex owner, Cecil Steigle, despite Kenny's repeated requests that she should. And he asked Ms Perry to send me affidavits for use in the writing of this book but she refused, saying, 'I think that's a bad idea.' A few days after that, he fired Jane Perry.

The Ohio State Public Defenders Office assigned him another lawyer, David Stebbins, to represent him in his appeals. This lawyer, as time would tell, was very friendly with William Kluge, one of Kenny's original defence lawyers, who several different people believed had been in collusion with the prosecution. Stebbins's friendship with Kluge became a point raised in later appeals by new lawyers for Kenny who essentially accused David Stebbins of refusing to raise the issue of the ineffectiveness of the trial counsel on Kenny's behalf because of his loyalty to Kluge. In the end, like Jane Perry's, Stebbins's days were numbered – in October 1992, he would resign from the Public Defenders Office after an investigation uncovered corruption and misappropriation of funds within the office.

By the end of June 1992, the British Foreign Office, having been under further pressure from Alistair Darling and other MPs, committed themselves to supporting Kenny should his appeals fail. Days later, Freedom Now decided to assist with Kenny's appeals. In conjunction with *This Week* producers and the editor of *The Mail on Sunday*, they convinced Clive Stafford-Smith to represent Kenny pro bono (without charge). Clive, a British lawyer working at the Southern Center for Human Rights in Atlanta, Georgia, had earned a reputation for being a 'death row expert' through his excellent record in helping to free condemned prisoners from death row. Clive decided to make no legal moves until the Ohio Supreme Court rendered their decision over the arguments Jane Perry had presented some months before.

Undoubtedly, Kenny's case was now receiving the kind of attention he needed. Thousands of letters poured in to him, many offering moral support, and, by mid July, the European Parliament demanded that the US retry Kenny. I believed this had to lead to the American media reporting Kenny's case. I also believed that the unanimous support shown towards him would persuade the Ohio Supreme Court to grant a retrial. Neither of these things happened.

On August the twelfth 1992, the Ohio Supreme Court rejected Kenny's appeal in a four-to-three decision in which three of the presiding seven judges had favoured overturning Kenny's conviction. Still, although sorely disappointed by the ruling against him, Kenny took comfort and hope from the fact that the decision hadn't been unanimous. Also, the court hadn't heard any of the new evidence, such as the affidavits Dad had collected, and Kenny believed that the decision would go the other way when this evidence was allowed to be heard.

Three weeks later, David Stebbins filed a motion for rehearing with the Ohio Supreme Court – a formality that always follows when a request for a retrial has been denied. On September the thirtieth, the court denied the motion and set an execution date to fall within sixty days. At this point, a Notice of Appeal to the United States Supreme Court was filed. This temporarily suspended Kenny's execution date.

It was at this stage that Clive Stafford-Smith, true to his word, stepped in. With Clive on board came rejuvenated hope for Kenny. Clive had greater resources at his disposal than the Public Defenders Office and courts are more inclined to listen to a successful lawyer like him than they are to the low-profile local lawyers in the Public Defenders Office. A lawyer in private practice, representing a convicted felon pro bono, generally receives the attention of the court because they consider that, logically, there has to be some merit to the case otherwise the lawyer wouldn't waste his time and his own money representing the prisoner.

However, despite Clive's appearance, Kenny doubted his appeal to the US Supreme Court would be a success. 'They never [accept a] review [of] a death penalty case until the post-conviction phase,' he wrote. This phase was only triggered when his direct appeal phase was exhausted by the US Supreme Court. It was going to take months to find out if Kenny's statement was correct – his appeal to the US Supreme Court would not be filed until March the third 1993.

In the meantime, two other matters distracted Kenny. The first concerned his health. The air-conditioning unit in death row filtered used air from the cellblock and recycled it but the air filter was ineffective against stopping micro-bacteria. Tuberculosis circulated through the unit, infecting several prisoners. It attacked Kenny and after the initial symptoms faded, it left him feeling drained and fatigued for many months. The infirmary prescribed him antibiotics that he had to take for a year. But the TB permanently scarred him, leaving him with dark sunken eyes.

The second distraction in Kenny's life was a woman. Among the letters of support he'd received and replied to, he became intimate with one writer – that is, as intimate as two people can become through letters. The young woman was a Dundee law student. Kenny hadn't mentioned the woman in any of his letters and I learned about her from a newspaper Mum sent. The tabloid article stated that the woman had pledged her undying love for Kenny or something to that affect and that she had proposed marriage to him. It sounded ridiculous. I could understand Kenny's infatuation given his loneliness and deprived circumstances, but her motive didn't become clear until a later article in the *Daily Record* revealed that the young woman was already married. Obviously, her motive had been to gain attention by having her name and face printed in the paper.

If Kenny had been hurt by this revelation, he didn't express it. In fact, a few months later, it was reported that he had become involved in another romantic relationship, this time with a twenty-eight-year-old in Aberdeen. This soap opera fizzled out too. As one psychologist, a Dr Ian Stephen, theorised in regard to Kenny's romances, as quoted in the *Daily Record*, 'I think he has been trying to cope with life via these various relationships. It's like he's clinging to life in the outside world – escaping from prison.'

As November passed and the media ban was lifted from Kenny, he gave a couple of interviews but not as many as he'd expected. The ban had probably been effective in knocking the wind out of the sails of those who had previously been scrambling for access to interview him. The demand for his story waned. However, the British media surfaced again on March the third 1993, when his appeal to the US Supreme Court was filed. But, three weeks after his appeal was filed, the US Supreme Court dismissed it.

In April, Clive then filed a motion for a rehearing but the court rejected this too. It was around this time that Clive realised Kenny's chances of a successful appeal would be strengthened if the resources and financial backing of a heavy-hitting law firm could be found. Clive simply couldn't dedicate the time Kenny's case needed because he was already juggling several other cases. One case in particular, that of another British man, convicted murderer Nicholas Ingram, necessitated a great deal of Clive's attention because his case was nearing its final stage of appeal and the executioner had begun warming his hands.

Within months, Clive gathered Kenny's case materials and approached Goodwin, Proctor & Hoar, the largest and most prestigious law firm in Boston, Massachusetts. The firm rarely agreed to consider taking on pro bono prisoner cases at such a late stage in the appellate process and it took them some time to make a decision about taking on Kenny's. Fortunately, Kenny had until April 1994 in which to file his first appeal to begin the final post-conviction stage of his appeals so time wasn't an enemy. This fresh round of appeals, the post-conviction phase, would begin at the Ohio Court of Appeals. This would be followed by the Ohio Supreme Court. If this failed, his appeal would enter the Federal District Court for the first time and, if it was denied there, the 6th Circuit Federal Court of Appeals would review his case. If they denied his appeal, his final court of appeal was the US Supreme Court. If this highest court in the land denied his appeal, Kenny would be executed without further delay.

Attorney Paul Nemser of Goodwin, Proctor & Hoar met with Clive. His law firm had successfully argued a Florida death row case in the 1980s and it so happened that they were looking for another similar challenge. They had already reviewed a list of over a hundred cases that they were considering taking up. Kenny's case interested him.

'There appeared to be a real chance Kenny was innocent,' Paul Nemser said. 'The more we learned, the more that was borne out.'

In late November 1993, Paul and another member of the firm, David Apfel, visited Kenny at the Southern Ohio Correctional

Facility to inform him personally that they had agreed to represent him and to discuss the case further. Kenny was immediately impressed – not only by their legal credentials but also by their expensive tailored suits and polished fingernails. They brought a previously overlooked pathologist's report of Cynthia Collins autopsy to his attention. The report found 'a little deposit of smoke and carbonatious material primarily on the left hand'. Smoke and carbonatious material are consistent with a burn from a match. In itself, this provided conclusive evidence she had not remained in her room during the fire because no evidence of the fire or matches, that could account for the deposit of carbonatious material on her hand, existed in her room.

The enthusiasm of the lawyers infected Kenny and he returned to his cell wearing a smile yet their proposed strategy left him concerned. Instead of immediately entering the post-conviction stage, his lawyers wanted to file a Murnahan Motion. This was a petition to the court that would argue, among other things, that Kenny's previous appeals had been presented by incompetent lawyers and, because of this, the court should allow the appeal process to start anew with his new lawyers who could now be deemed competent. No one on Ohio's death row had ever won a Murnahan Motion so Kenny considered it a waste of time. Their strategy would extend his appeal process and extend his time on death row. He began an inner debate about whether he should agree to give his lawyers the go ahead. 'I had already served six years on death row and I was sick of it all,' Kenny said.

The goal of his lawyers in trying to restart the appellate process was that it would give them the opportunity to present arguments that should have been raised originally but were not. The failure to raise a specific argument during the first stage of appeal barred Kenny's lawyers from raising the argument later, in the post-conviction stage. Also, if the court granted the Murnahan Motion, Kenny's lawyers would have a ninety-day opportunity to file a motion for a hearing to request a new trial. At this hearing, they would be permitted to introduce all of the new evidence.

In the week after his meeting with the lawyers, Kenny received a letter from Paul, saying:

> Kenny, please understand that, if at any point in this process you disagree with something we are doing, or have ideas regarding other avenues we should be following, you should let us know. You are the boss. This case is your life, and I want you to be an active participant and partner in the defence. This is not to say that we will simply accept any idea you present. We will, however, consider everything. We will tell you when your ideas are great, and if they are not so great, we will tell you that as well. None of us, including you, can be overly sensitive if an idea or suggestion is rejected. We don't want anything, especially petty sensitivities or fragile egos, to stand in the way of forging the best defence we can.

This paragraph ended Kenny's debate. He was caught by Paul's honesty and sincerity. They were focused to win, not waste time, and he decided to keep his reservations over the Murnahan Motion to himself.

In April 1994, the Murnahan Motion was filed at the Ohio Court of Appeals. This court would not disappoint in taking its time to render its decision over the merits of this new motion – it took ten months. During this time, Paul Nemser handed Kenny's case over to his partner, forty-three-year-old attorney Ken Parsigian, who was one of the top criminal specialists in the firm. Ken Parsigian went to work. He retained two of the top international arson experts – Dr David Hoover from the University of Akron and Richard Custer from Quincy,

Massachusetts. (Mr Custer had been the arson expert featured in the *Los Angeles Times* article about the 'flashover' phenomenon Kenny had read.) Both men began reviewing the samples and other materials related to Kenny's case. While they conducted their investigations and tests on the materials, Kim Gray, an investigator for Goodwin, Proctor & Hoar, headed for Ohio.

Kim interviewed Peggy Price who revealed that, when she had spoken to Kenny's trial defence lawyers, Kluge and Donahue, she told them about Cynthia's habit of playing with matches and lighters. Kluge's failure to bring this up at trial remains totally inexplicable. Peggy also again admitted, 'I was very nervous during Kenny's trial and said what I thought the lawyers wanted to hear. I know for a fact that I never heard Kenny Richey say he was going to burn anything or use marine corps tactics.'

More importantly, Kim spoke with Larry Frazier. Mr Frazier had taken over from Sherry Tice as the apartment complex manager on July the first, the day after the fire. He told Kim that he started repair work on Hope Collins's balcony deck ten days after the fire. On July the tenth or the eleventh, he *replaced* the deck's railing and the charred boards from the deck, then he covered the deck using oil-based stain. Later, he cleaned his brushes on the deck using paint thinner. If Larry Frazier's date is correct, it means that, when Cryer had taken samples from the deck on July the seventeenth, the samples he got were from a new deck and not from the deck that had been charred and burned. He had, therefore, apparently lied when he'd sworn he had taken samples from the charred area of the balcony as the charred material had already been removed. But why would he lie? Probably to avoid having to admit that this was yet another area of evidence collection that had been mishandled and bungled.

Further good news materialised as a result of Dr Hoover and Mr Custer's investigations. Regarding the woodchip from the patio balcony on which evidence of paint thinner was found, paint thinner is an extremely volatile substance and, according to Mr Custer, it is extraordinarily unlikely that any trace of paint thinner splashed on to the patio balcony to start the fire could be found seventeen or eighteen days later. Dr Hoover concurred with this and he maintains that it is far more likely that the trace of paint thinner was applied to the patio balcony much closer in time to July the seventeenth than to the day of the fire on June the thirtieth. After fully reviewing all of the evidence, Mr Custer formed the following opinion:

> It is just as, if not more, likely that the June thirtieth fire was caused by the careless discard of smoking materials or child's play than the fire was caused by arson. Robert Cryer's opinion offered at trial is based on unsound scientific principles that are not accepted in the forensic science community for the investigation of arson-related fires.

Ken Parsigian then obtained the services of the top certified professional chemist in the United States, Andrew I. Armstrong PhD, the owner and president of the Armstrong Forensic Laboratory in Texas. Like Mr Custer and Dr Hoover, Dr Armstrong's credentials were impeccable – he had received a host of awards, including the President's Award for 'Exemplary Standards and Professionalism in Forensic Chemistry'. He was the author of nineteen publications and lectured extensively throughout the United States. His findings were unexpected and shocking. He found that Sample Seven, the woodchips taken from the patio balcony, actually tested negative for identifiable liquids. 'Paint thinner cannot be identified in the recovery, based on the 1986 or current scientific criteria. There is a reasonable probability the recovery of Sample Seven is turpentine indigenous to the wood used to construct the patio balcony.'

Regarding Sample Five, the carpet cutting that was found by

the Ohio State Forensic Lab to have traces of petrol on it, Dr Armstrong found:

> Sample Five should be reported as negative for identifiable flammable liquids based on the current scientific criteria. Even if 1986 criteria are used, the 1986 report should have stated that the recovery in Sample Five was consistent with a low level of evaporated gasoline. The lack of structure means that, if Sample Five is gasoline, it is evaporated gasoline. It is impossible to determine whether the gasoline was on the carpet before the carpet was placed in the dump or on the sheriff's parking lot.

Regarding Sample Four, the carpet cutting that the Ohio lab claimed to have had paint thinner on it, Dr Armstrong found:

> Sample Four contains a low level of a medium petroleum distillate that cannot be positively identified as paint thinner. The recovery of Sample Four is more consistent with ordinary household products, such as furniture polish or insecticides.

Furthermore, regarding the balcony woodchip paint thinner sample and the carpet paint thinner sample, Dr Armstrong found:

> The relative intensity of the branched hydrocarbons from the recovery from Sample Four do not correspond to the pattern of information from Sample Seven. Therefore, the recovery from Sample Seven and Sample Four are not the same substance.

Based on the findings of these top experts in their respective fields, there was no valid evidence to suggest that the fire in Hope Collins's apartment was caused by arson. Of the nine samples taken from the fire scene, not one tested positive for paint thinner or petrol. What's clear is that the forensic evidence used to convict Kenny was incorrect but whether or not this evidence was, in fact, fabricated remains a matter for speculation. As Kenny wrote, 'I feel vindicated by the findings. It proves that the concerted actions of Basinger and Cryer, to name but two, were a calculated attempt to use the American justice system as a tool to legally commit murder against me.' A sharp accusation, for sure, but, given Dr Armstrong's findings, it isn't one that can easily be dismissed as just the words of a bitter man.

However, if Kenny expected release from death row as a result of the findings, he was mistaken. New evidence, such as Dr Armstrong's findings, is rarely allowed to be introduced during the post-conviction phase of a prisoner's appeal. With only a few exceptions, procedural rules dictate that new evidence can only be introduced during the initial phase of appeals.

In January 1995, the Ohio Court of Appeals denied his Murnahan Motion, as Kenny had feared, and the court set a new date for his execution to take place in sixty days. On February the sixteenth, his lawyers appealed the denial of the Murnahan Motion to the Ohio Supreme Court. The action postponed Kenny's date of execution pending the outcome of the new motion.

Kenny tried to remain optimistic but it was difficult because he had absolutely no faith in the American legal system. He couldn't understand why, after an abundance of evidence which showed his innocence, the courts wouldn't step in and make things right. Even his move to a new death row facility, built in the high-tech multi-million-dollar Mansfield Correctional Institution, only an hour's drive from Columbus Grove, failed to make things easier despite its perks – his cell was larger and it contained a shower, in addition to the toilet and sink, and he was allowed twenty-one hours a week exercise outside and daily phone calls (albeit reverse-charge calls only). It was still a prison. It was still death row, a human slaughterhouse. He spent much of his time trying to escape via his black-and-white telly.

But, due to the number of legal programmes like *Cops* and *Law and Order*, watching the telly usually only reminded him of his own predicament. Then there was the infamous OJ Simpson trial. It captivated him just as it did the rest of America. Despite the man's seemingly obvious guilt, OJ Simpson sat with his expensive legal team who dodged and weaved through a trial that lasted months. Kenny was tried and convicted in three days – poor man's justice.

And the telly reminded him of another Briton, Nick Ingram, who was represented by Clive Stafford-Smith. Not that Nick Ingram's case received much publicity – just a short mention on the news. Although Ingram had lived in the United States since he was a toddler, he had been born in the UK and was officially British. No Briton had been executed in the United States in modern times. This changed on April the eighth 1995. After twelve years on Georgia's death row, Nick Ingram left prison in a hearse. 'I'd have a public execution in the town square every Sunday,' one of the demonstrators was quoted as saying as Ingram's hearse rolled by. 'It's the best deterrent of all.' The statement reflected the general attitude of Americans, an ignorance Kenny found no solace in.

Following the execution, Kenny's case surfaced in the British press again. If Kenny's appeals failed, he would be the next Briton to be executed. Clive Stafford-Smith, working together with the Goodwin, Proctor & Hoar lawyers, publicly pledged to save Kenny. 'But [Prime Minister] Major's got to help this time,' the *Daily Record* quoted him as saying. 'Kenny needs the Prime Minister to show a little backbone and get involved in the case.'

A spokesman for Downing Street offered a carrot. 'If a direct approach is made, the Prime Minister will look at the individual circumstances.'

Days later, Mum wrote to the Prime Minister, seeking help. On May the twenty-third, Downing Street's Private Secretary, Edward Oakden, replied. He stated that the British government had no standing in Kenny's case. 'We have considered very carefully whether there are any grounds on which an appeal might be made by the British government. I am sorry to tell you that we have concluded that there are not.'

Downing Street's response was another disappointment for Kenny. With each disappointment, his resistance crumbled and, in a moving letter, he wrote:

> As each day comes and goes, bit by bit, another piece of me dies while I silently weep at its loss. With each new appeal, my hopes are raised that the court will finally right a wrong but all that results is despair as each court continually upholds my conviction and sentence of death. I no longer feel like the person I used to be. I feel like a boxer in the fifteenth round of a beating and I try to stay on my feet with each blow that comes. Still, a voice from deep within tells me to carry on and keep fighting, no matter what. As difficult as it's been these past nine years, somehow I manage to go on . . . hoping.

In July 1995, the Ohio Supreme Court accepted Kenny's Murnahan Motion and ordered a full review of his case. Letters from Kenny expressed his first signs of genuine optimism. 'I believe this is it, Tom,' he wrote. 'I know the decision means they're only reviewing my case and they haven't made any decisions but how can they ignore what has happened? They last decided narrowly four-to-three against me but now, with them reviewing my case fully, all I need is one more judge to open his eyes.'

In August 1995, the Ohio Supreme Court, after fully reviewing Kenny's case, upheld his conviction and the decisions of the previous appeals in a six-to-one judgement. I didn't hear from

Kenny for a couple of months and, when he did write, his words were the whispers of a dying man. For the first time, he sounded defeated, accepting of his fate.

The heavy ash-wood chair remains at Lucasville inside a red-brick building known as the Death House. Within the next few years, Ohio would join other US states in casting aside its twenty-year unofficial moratorium on executions. Twenty-four hours before they were due to be executed, condemned inmates began being transported from Mansfield to the Death House.

'I don't want to die,' Kenny said, 'but I will if it means dying for what I believe in. I believe in standing up for myself and standing by the truth and, if I die for fighting for that, then so be it. At least I'll die knowing I did everything to prove my innocence. Death comes to us all in the end but I'll know I died an innocent man.'

'Have you ever been in the dark . . . then a little ray of light comes and you begin to see?'

James Richey, speaking of Karen Torley

13

A RAY OF LIGHT

By chance, in 1995, an unemployed single mother of four, Karen Torley, read an article about Kenny in the *Glasgow Herald*. She had seen the Thames TV programme, *This Week*, a few years earlier but she hadn't been impressed. 'I thought he was an arrogant man who was probably guilty,' she said of her feelings at the time. But reading the newspaper article in 1995 had a different effect on her. 'Something about the whole thing made me totally disturbed,' she said.

Up to this point, the thirty-four years of Karen Torley's life had been pretty unremarkable. The eldest of four children, she grew up in a middle-class family and, after finishing school, she got married at the age of eighteen and, by the age of twenty-five, she had had four children. She separated from her husband several years later and, in 1995, she was living on the dole in a two-storey tenement in Cambuslang, South Glasgow. She was the last person anyone would suspect could make a difference in Kenny's life.

Three weeks after Karen read the article about Kenny, she couldn't shake the story from her mind. 'Here was this man, a Scot, thousands of miles from home, going to be executed by a foreign country.' She wrote Kenny a letter and, to her surprise, he wrote back. He asked her if she would pen a few letters on his behalf, including one to Ohio's Supreme Court. For some reason and even she's not sure why, she did.

I didn't know about Karen Torley until a couple of months after she first wrote to Kenny. She got in touch with me to ask for a copy of the manuscript I'd written about Kenny's case as she thought it would help her to understand his situation better. My immediate reaction was to roll my eyes and think, 'Not another one!' I suspected she was another woman who was only briefly getting involved because she wanted her face in the paper. Still, I sent Karen a copy of the manuscript and also a thorny letter expressing my suspicions and questioning her motives. The last thing Kenny needed was another attention seeker pledging her undying love for him in the bloody newspaper.

My letter elicited the fiery response I wanted. After an initial tirade – 'You don't know me so you shouldn't judge me!' type of thing – Karen's tone softened. 'I want to understand his case better and help if I can.' I had to admit that Karen had the right kind of pushy attitude a person needed to lead a campaign on Kenny's behalf.

Over the ensuing months, the more Karen read about Kenny's case, the more she questioned the validity of the conviction and the more she wanted to help. Yet, she didn't know how to proceed. She wrote to the obvious places, like the court, many times over and she took offence at the lack of response. She couldn't understand how the American officials she contacted could be so indifferent when an apparently innocent man's life hung in the balance. But, instead of giving up, it just strengthened her resolve.

She realised that more needed to be done. Her ultimate aim was to secure a new trial for Kenny. This was really something only his lawyers could achieve but, to help them score that goal, they could do with a pass or even a dribble – and some positive support from the public and influential people might just help them to get into the penalty box. Around this time, the

British press had not been so positive so she began calling and writing letters to British reporters in an effort to cultivate relationships with them. As a result, articles appeared more frequently and what they contained grew more positive.

The turning point in her fledgling campaign happened in 1996. Sister Helen Prejean had written *Dead Man Walking*, a book about her relationship with a prisoner on death row. The book led to an Oscar winning-performance from Susan Sarandon who played Sister Helen in the movie of the same name. Sister Helen had been invited to Glasgow University to address a group of law students and lawyers and one of the reporters Karen was in contact with asked her if she'd like to attend the event. She was told that there might be a chance for her to talk to the audience after Sister Helen had delivered her speech. Karen was terrified. She had never spoken to a large group of educated people and she was self-conscious about her strong Glasgow accent. Still, a man's life was at stake. She dressed smartly in a blue blazer and yellow blouse, got in a taxi to the university and took up a position at the rear of the auditorium.

Sister Helen talked for over an hour. She was mesmerising, Karen recalled, but she assumed there would be no time left for her. Then she heard her name called. As she walked on unstable legs to the stage, she thought, 'What am I doing here, talking to these educated people? They can hear my heart pounding, my legs shaking, my teeth chattering.'

Karen remembers little of her talk. She only remembers that the organisers told her she had made a good impression. Afterwards, she was surrounded by reporters asking her for interviews. And the students donated nearly £100 towards Karen's fund to fly Mum over to visit Kenny. 'From then on, people started to take me seriously,' Karen said.

Running the campaign on small donations and with the British press now on her side, Karen shifted her focus to try to gain the support of the British government and other prominent officials.

Kenny's citizenship remained a problem. Karen discovered that Kenny had voted in two national elections and was eligible for national health insurance. English lawyer, Andrew McCooey, got involved with the citizenship issue. It led to the law firm, Lovells, agreeing to represent Kenny and Karen pro bono. Kenny's case, amongst others, was used by Lord Averbury to push through an amendment to change British law to allow the children of British mothers, rather than just the children of fathers, to become eligible for British citizenship. In 2003, Kenny, who was born in Zeist, Holland, was the first to be officially granted citizenship under the new law.

For months in 1996, Karen harangued prominent officials and her persistence led to support from Glenda Jackson, the Member of Parliament and Oscar-winning actress. Ms Jackson wrote to the Ohio Attorney General, Betty Montgomery, requesting a new trial for Kenny. However, the response was typical – 'A qualified court and jury already have found Mr Richey guilty of murder.'

Karen understood that the pro-Richey momentum in Britain would mean more if she could open doors in the United States, particularly in Ohio. She realised the challenge she faced first hand when she travelled to Ohio in November 1996 with a film crew from the ITV programme, *World In Action*. She participated in a phone-in radio show in Lima. The callers trashed Kenny and ridiculed Karen for supporting a 'child killer'. She found little sympathy in Putnam County either. Karen said, 'It seemed like these people were so brainwashed by their trust in their government and their legal system, that they believe it can't possibly make a mistake. They can't get beyond their blind faith in order to open their eyes to the facts that show Kenny's innocence.'

During her trip to Ohio, prison officials denied her visitation with Kenny. 'I think that was payback,' she said. She met our dad and Steven while in Ohio and she met Kenny's lawyer, Ken Parsigian, who, in June of 1996, had filed the latest petition to the Court of Appeals, thus beginning Kenny's last stage of appeals – the post-conviction phase.

In 1997, the appeal to the Ohio Court of Appeals would be decided by three judges, one of whom had been on the panel of judges who had convicted Kenny. Apparently, the American courts saw no conflict of interest there. The appellate judges refused to admit the new evidence and accepted the argument, presented by Prosecutor Gershultz, that 'even though the new evidence may establish Richey's innocence, the Ohio and US constitutions nonetheless allow him to be executed because the prosecution did not know [at the time of the trial] that the scientific testimony offered at trial was false and unreliable.'

It was shocking. They admitted Kenny may be innocent but upheld the decision to execute him anyway. The decision only cemented Karen's determination and provided further evidence of Ohio's willingness to murder an innocent man.

However, in 1998, Prosecutor Gershultz contacted Kenny's former attorney, William Kluge, who, in turn, contacted Ken Parsigian with a proposal. He suggested that, if Kenny would agree to a transfer to a Scottish prison under the international transfer treaty, Ohio authorities were willing to let him go, even if Scottish authorities wanted to release him that same day – as long as Kenny agreed to withdraw his appeals and never to return to the United States again.

A guilty man would accept the deal. Even some innocent men would accept the deal. Kenny didn't.

Footnote: Credit must be given to the *Toledo Blade* whose article, written by George Tanber, was of assistance in the writing of this chapter.

14

NO DEALS

I thought Kenny was daft for rejecting a deal that would give him his freedom. For as much as he'd complained about the difficulties of life on death row, why wouldn't he snatch freedom from the hand of Gershultz? I wrote to Kenny and told him he was crazy.

He tried to explain, saying:

> I know it must seem daft, Tom, but they've taken so much from me and from our family. I couldn't walk down the street and have people point and say, 'There goes that man who got off scot-free from death row for murdering that wee lassie.' I just couldn't live with that. I couldn't live without exposing the lynching that happened in that courtroom in January 1987.
>
> I've made my share of mistakes in life and I haven't been the nicest person at times but I didn't start the fire that killed Cynthia. I didn't do it and I'm going to stand by that even if it means they'll execute me. I know it's hard to understand but what kind of man would I be if I didn't stand by my principles? People have willingly died for less . . . People will believe I'm guilty and people will believe in my innocence but there's one thing none of them will disagree about – I'm not a coward.

Despite this explanation, despite his willingness to stay on death row, he would still bemoan the treatment and conditions of prison – and those didn't improve after a riot on death row in 1997. Kenny tells how he had been sitting in his cell when it started. He was halfway through replying to a letter from Karen Torley when the block's sirens sounded. This wasn't unusual – inmates often set them off while trying to heat water in their cells – so he ignored them. About a minute later, Kenny heard banging coming from the cell above his. Its current occupant was a short, thin black man who went by the name of 'Pee-Wee'. Seconds later, Pee-Wee tumbled down the metal stairs, scrambled to his feet and ran towards the cell-block door, pursued by two other inmates. He couldn't get out because the door was locked and the guards had deserted the cell block. Pee-Wee tried to protect himself by backing into a closet but the two inmates came at him with chains and a padlock and beat him until he collapsed.

Old scores were often settled in this way. However, as Kenny told me in a letter, this was to erupt into something much bigger and, after leaving Pee-Wee unconscious, the two inmates rushed back upstairs.

> Then they began letting the inmates on both sides of the block out. They all came down to my level and then a few opened Lorraine's cell and gave him a beating. Some went back upstairs and opened Barry's cell and he got the worst beating of any of them.

All the cells were opened and inmates began trashing the block.

> I stood in front of my cell door and just watched – as did most of the other guys. I took no part in any of it. I spent the next few hours sitting in my cell or just out in front of it with my best friend and a couple of other mates. One of my

friends, Jason Robb, was one of the main people involved in the Lucasville riot of 1993 and he asked me and Robert Vanhook to come over to sit in his cell as there would be safety in numbers. So we stocked up on coffee and some smokes and went to his cell. [Shortly after that,] all hell broke loose. We had locked ourselves in Jason's cell. Everyone else had also locked up by this time. I was sitting on the bunk when the window of the cell exploded, sending glass every-where. Two canisters of tear gas flew in and filled the place with smoke. I couldn't breathe. My lungs felt like they were being crushed in a vice. My eyes and skin burned We couldn't get out as we'd locked the cell door. Jason and Robert started heaving and moved to the window to try to get some air but, just as they did, a guard outside the window said, 'Get the fuck away from the window, you pieces of shit!' And then he sprayed them with mace.

I had a folded blanket clutched to my face in an attempt to avoid breathing the gas and I was lying on the floor at the cell door. Over the next twenty-five minutes, the guards tossed thirteen more canisters of tear gas into the cell. I later learned from the other inmates that their cells had only been hit with one, two or, at most, three canisters.

About forty minutes later, guards arrived at the cell door and ordered Kenny, Jason and Robert to strip to their briefs and stand facing the far wall. After they complied, the guards burst into the cell, pulled all three of them to the floor and cuffed their hands behind their backs.

They beat the shit out of us. One guard stomped once on my head and once on my face, then stood on my face, ground his boot into my face and then kicked me in the face. Meanwhile, his fellow guards stomped on my bare feet, on my legs and kicked me in the ribs. Another one knelt on my back and

190

sprayed a whole can of mace into my face. My skin actually blistered. The next day, it peeled and caused a dozen open sores in spots where the skin had come off the most.

They beat the crap out of all three of us but Jason got the worst of it. They fractured his skull. He had to go to Ohio State University hospital he was so bad. The guards finally lifted us up and led us out of the building where we were handed to regular guards (the guards who stormed the block were Special Weapons and Tactics guards).

Of over two hundred death row inmates, only a token thirty-six were removed from death row. Kenny and the other prisoners were taken to a maintenance building where highway patrol police took photographs of them. A nurse briefly looked them over and they were dressed in orange overalls. Then they had to lie on their stomachs, on a cold cement floor, with their hands cuffed behind their backs.

They kept us like that for five bloody hours. At first, they wouldn't even let us go to the bathroom so two inmates pissed themselves where they lay, Ten minutes later, some of the guards who stormed our block came and took a few of us to the toilet. The two who took me punched me and pushed me and one smashed his elbow right into my mouth, knocking a tooth loose. They actually said that, if they wanted to, they could make sure I ended up 'like that whore of a princess' of mine and called me 'a British piece of shit'. They said they could kill me and that they really wanted to. They beat me in front of everyone, including the sergeant and a nurse. The latter never said anything – they just sat there.

Eventually, Kenny and the other inmates were led to another building. Each inmate had his shoes taken away and was placed in a cell with no mattress, no pillow, no sheets. Over the following days, as calm returned, basic items were issued but it would be several months before the thirty-six inmates were allowed back to death row. Kenny says of this time, 'This was just another storm on the journey to justice and freedom and I weathered it just as I did the rest.'

As public attention increased in Kenny's case and the prison routinely received a barrage of calls from the British press, what Kenny noticed most was the change in the attitudes of several guards who worked regularly on death row. They seemed to resent the prying from the 'foreign press'. Kenny tried to avoid communicating with them as much as possible but sometimes it was necessary and they didn't try to hide their venomous demeanours.

According to Kenny, one guard in particular openly loathed him. His name was Sergeant Duda. Karen and Mum had put together a food package and mailed it to Kenny – death row prisoners were allowed one package a year. It had been filled with Kenny's favourite goodies – Yorkie bars, Jamaican Rum bars, Smarties, shortbread, Scotch whisky fudge etc. Sergeant Duda had been passing out the food boxes and, as he rolled his cart by Kenny's cell, Kenny asked about his food box. Duda told him he'd get it shortly, in a day or two. A week later, Kenny again asked about his box. Duda then claimed he hadn't received a box for him. Kenny knew it was a lie. Mum had sent the box a month before with adequate postage and it had been properly addressed.

Over the next two months, Kenny complained about not receiving his box. Initially, Duda and the rest of the prison staff had claimed that no box for Kenny had arrived but then he was told that a box had arrived for him but it had to be returned because it hadn't been properly addressed. Three months later, Mum received the box back. When she opened it, half of its contents had been eaten and the empty wrappers had been tossed back in the box.

Some prison staff, particularly in death row, work and act with impunity. They live in two worlds – the world outside prison and the world in prison. They often wear different faces depending on which world they're in at the time. In prison, they can take out their aggression without fear of retribution and many do. Few care about death row inmates. They are human refuse, dead men walking, and many guards treat them as such. Oddly, only when the American press began to question Kenny's conviction in 1998, beginning with one of the respected and usually pro death penalty newspapers, *The Toledo Blade*, did Kenny notice a change in the guards' attitude. 'They acted more civil,' Kenny wrote. 'But I don't know if this was because they respected me more or if it was because they feared that maybe I would say something about them?'

In 1998, one prisoner took exception to the interest Kenny's case was receiving in Ohio. He was a young man, no more than twenty-one years old. He'd only recently arrived on death row and he was mad at the world. He turned his aggression on Kenny. Kenny wrote:

> I never saw it coming. I was in the recreation cage and I got hit from behind, then the fight was on. We exchanged blows and, like most fights, we went to the ground. The guards yelled at us to break it up while other prisoners in the cage watched but the guards wouldn't enter the cage. They had to wait for back up. I was losing my wind so I put the youngster in a choke-hold. He tried to jamb his fingers in my eye so I moved my head and his fingers went into my mouth. I bit down on them. It was too much pressure for my front tooth which broke completely but the gum held in place.

When the guards entered the cage and separated the two, Kenny felt as if he was being stabbed in the heart. The physical exertion had been too much for him and he was having a heart attack. Prison staff rushed him to hospital. When he came to later that evening, his front tooth was gone.

His heart attack wasn't just a physical blow – it also affected him mentally. He said, 'It was a blow to my ego, I admit that. I mean, I was only thirty-four years old. I had put on some weight but I didn't realise I'd gotten so out of shape.'

He tried to lose weight with exercise but, over the following years, his weight only increased. He didn't know at the time that he'd contracted diabetes. He'd been more concerned with his tooth. He sought a replacement from the prison dentist but the man apparently saw no point in wasting resources on a death row inmate and rebuffed Kenny's requests.

Vanity spurred creativity. Kenny used one of the white plastic food tray spoons to make a tooth. He trimmed it to size using nail clippers then smoothed the edges using a nail file. He then attached a small wire at the top and melted it on to the back. Anchored by the wire to his two neighbouring teeth, the replacement fitted snugly. As long as he didn't push the tooth with his tongue, it stayed in place but, of course, it stood out like a whiteboard between a row of tombstones.

As 1998 passed into 1999 and 1999 became the year 2000, Kenny's campaign continued to build through Karen's leadership. She still ran it on a shoestring budget, from a corner of her bedroom in Cambuslang, but, with the increase in computer networking through the 1990s, Karen had managed to reach people in other corners of the world and, by this time, an international army of support backed Kenny. Amnesty International took an interest and declared Kenny's case the 'most compelling case of innocence on death row'. British politicians got more involved. Margo MacDonald MSP obtained Kenny's court transcripts and had them examined by Scotland's most senior lawyers. 'They concluded that the evidence presented in the trial was completely unfounded and would never have been accepted in a Scottish court,' she said. Celebrities, such as Susan

Sarandon, Robbie Coltrane and Irvine Welsh, also pledged support and even the late Pope John Paul II urged the United States to retry Kenny. Yet, none of this momentum seemed to sway the Ohio courts. They continued to reject Kenny's appeals and motions.

Kenny descended into another depressive state as the fight wore him down. The letters I got from him were few and far between. He got burned out on writing. 'I just ran out of things to write about mostly,' he explained. 'After a while, I didn't even want to pick up a pen. I didn't want to share my misery with others any more.' Life dragged on just as it had done in the years before.

Early in 2003, his lawyers filed an appeal to the 6th Circuit Court of Appeals. It would be his last realistic opportunity for appellate review. If they rejected the appeal, Kenny knew he'd hear the footsteps of the executioner walking to the death house. He would be able to file one more appeal, to the United States Supreme Court but this highest court in the land only agreed to hear a small percentage of the thousands of desperate last-ditch efforts it received each session.

Later that year, the producers from the American TV programme, *American Justice*, took an interest in Kenny's case. It was the first and only major American film crew to visit Kenny in all the years. They investigated the case and interviewed Kenny. They made a convincing case questioning his conviction. But what bothered me while viewing the programme was seeing Kenny. The man who appeared on the programme was not the young slim brother I knew. Truth is, when I saw Kenny, I mistook him for another death row prisoner who was being interviewed about Kenny. Overweight, he sat with stooping shoulders, his face looking like a ball of dough, with two pinholes for eyes. When he talked, he barely moved his lips and then I realised it must be in an effort to avoid displaying his plastic tooth. 'What happened to my brother?' were the words that surfaced in my mind. Life on death row had beaten him down. When the programme ended, guilt was the main feeling in my bag of emotions. I had been partly responsible for the brother I no longer recognised.

In December, a couple of months after Kenny was interviewed by *American Justice*, a nurse checked Kenny's glucose level. It was around 480. The normal range for a person is between 80 and 120. The nurse rechecked it. She immediately strode to the telephone. Within the hour, Kenny was rushed to the infirmary and he spent the weekend there. He received a shot of insulin every four hours for three days until his glucose level decreased to the normal range. Diabetes explained why he had often felt fatigued and why he had put on so much weight – both were down to his body's inefficiency in burning sugar which had turned it to fat.

He saw the New Year in, as usual, with a cup of tea in hand and bagpipes playing from his tape deck. It offered no more promise than the seventeen New Years before it. In February, Alistair Carmichael MP and Amnesty International's Kate Allen visited Kenny. They were taken aback by Kenny's chains. Although in a separate booth, the guards insisted on keeping Kenny's hands chained to his waist and his legs shackled to a D-ring bolted to the floor. They frowned as Kenny talked. One of his teeth looked extremely white. Then, as Kenny grinned, the tooth popped forward, yawning like a garage door. Kenny reacted with obvious embarrassment and covered his mouth while he refitted the tooth. Carmichael and Kate Allen reacted with anger. Following the visit, they contacted the prison warden who assured them that Kenny would be fitted with a dental retainer. He never was.

When Carmichael returned to the UK, he raised a Commons Motion that backed Kenny's claims of innocence and it was signed by 150 MPs. In March, Chris Mullin, the Junior Foreign Office Minister, said the British government was doing all it could to prevent Kenny's execution. MP Carmichael said, 'I hope the government will get involved in the Supreme Court hearing itself. They have the power to file a brief, which is basically just writing to the court giving the government's thoughts on it. Basically, anyone who has a statable interest can file a brief as a friend of the court. Given that Kenny is a British citizen, the government would have a statable interest.'

Everyone still waited for the decision from the 6th Circuit Court of Appeals. A year had passed since they had retired and their decision was expected any day. Kenny had stopped investing in hope long ago. Karen Torley told one reporter from *The Guardian*:

> He's been in there for eighteen years and he doesn't do optimism. Even the prosecution admits our evidence is better than theirs but the American constitution means you can still be executed if you had a supposedly fair trial even though the evidence proves Kenny is innocent. When Kenny's down, he'll say, 'I know they're going to kill me.' How can they even think of executing a man based on no evidence? And he'll let them, the stubborn bastard.

However, in the third week of April, Ken Parsigian received a call from the prosecutor's office. The prosecutor offered a deal. He agreed to drop the murder conviction if Kenny would acknowledge his guilt for the arson, meaning Kenny would be released for time served. Ken relayed the offer to Kenny. Kenny didn't hesitate. 'Tell him to go to hell.'

Several days after the prosecutor's offer, the 6th Circuit made a decision. In an unofficial ruling, the court sent Kenny's case back to the Ohio Supreme Court. The 6th Circuit suggested that the State judges reconsider Kenny's case because it appeared the prosecutors broke the law when they tried Kenny for a capital crime under the doctrine of transferred intent. Under the law of Ohio at the time, the doctrine of transferred intent could not support a capital murder offence. Of course, under this doctrine, prosecutors had argued that Kenny's intent was to kill Candy Barchet and Mike Nichols but ended up killing Cynthia Collins and, therefore, was guilty of aggravated felony murder because someone died. The 6th Circuit went on to state that condemning Kenny on ineligible grounds would violate his rights. They suggested that Kenny be tried again or released.

It put the Ohio Supreme Court judges in a quandary. If they retried Kenny, all the new evidence that they hadn't allowed to be introduced would be admissible and they would clearly lose their conviction. But the Ohio court didn't have to agree to either suggestion by the federal court. They could uphold their decision and return the case to the 6th Circuit. In which case, they would take the chance that the 6th Circuit would make an official ruling based on their previous suggestion.

Kenny took the news without emotion. 'I'm numb to it all, Tom. I'm tired of the courts dragging things out. I'm not twenty-one any more – I'm forty. I've lost most of my life – the part that counts anyway.'

In late June, however, Kenny's mood changed. 'The Ohio Supreme Court ignored the 6th Circuit and returned my case to them,' he wrote. 'Last night, I had a dream about being home. Do you know how long it's been since I've had a dream about being home? It was so vivid. For the first time for as long as I can remember, I can no longer feel the cold shadow of the executioner.'

My anger was originally vented on William Kluge but, since then, I have realised how flawed the US justice system is and so I don't feel so much animosity towards him as I do pity. It's just a shame that he wasted all that money going to law school and ended up being the plumber who blocked all the pipes.

James Richey

15

A MATTER OF HONOUR

In the weeks following the informal decision by the Federal 6th Circuit Court of Appeals, Kenny's hopes were lifted higher when he learned that the British law firm, Lovells, was acting on his behalf and on the behalf of over 200 British MPs to intervene as *amici curiae* (friends of the court). Lovells had been the firm that accepted Kenny's case pro bono, through Karen Torley, to successfully challenge UK nationality law, which resulted in Kenny being officially granted UK citizenship. As a result of this grant of nationality, Lovells were now able to prepare a petition on behalf of government MPs. The petition stated concerns over the safety of the conviction.

It was a rare move by the British government but anyone with a statable interest can file a petition as a 'friend of the court' and, given that Kenny was now a British citizen, the UK government had a statable interest in him. The brief was, in fact, only the second time the British government had formally stepped in to help a British citizen charged with a crime in the US and the first time the British government had become involved with a death penalty case. It was a credit to the diligence of Karen Torley for keeping Kenny's case on the conscience of those in positions of influence.

After the Ohio Supreme Court rejected the 6th Circuit's recommendation that they retry Kenny or free him because of the legally questionable murder conviction based on transferred intent, common sense would dictate that the 6th Circuit judges would then quickly reach a formal decision to order Kenny's release or retrial. However, common sense would also dictate that an appellate court would have seen fit to overturn Kenny's conviction at some point during his years on death row. After all, over two dozen appeals and motions had been filed, each containing enough overwhelming evidence to raise reasonable doubt over the strength of his conviction. But the 6th Circuit made no quick decision. To begin with, expectations were high but, slowly, time eroded Kenny's hopes. No matter how many times he'd experienced the waiting game, it didn't make things easier. By October 2004, his frustration was obvious in a letter to me. He wrote:

Still no news from the court yet as bloody usual. This is past being ridiculous. They should have given me a decision by now. This is definitely being dragged out intentionally. The [6th Circuit Court] judges already reviewed all the issues before their [informal] decision. I'm wondering if they're trying to find a way to back out of their questions regarding transferred intent so they can uphold my conviction. It wouldn't surprise me. What gets to me the most, besides the waiting, is my powerlessness to do anything to make them rule quicker. That's something I can never make anyone understand until they've been in a situation like this.

I watched that film, *The Matrix*, on the telly the other night and a scene really epitomised the past eighteen years of my life. It's when they have Neo (Keanu Reeves) in a room and his lips suddenly stick together and he fights to stretch them apart. He gets up from the table, trying to speak, and he's wrestled down by the bad guys in suits and sunglasses. It's been like that for me for as long I can remember. And I'm bitter, Tom, I'm so damn bitter. They just refuse to listen to me and refuse to do what's right because it would mean they'd have to acknowledge their mistakes which would undermine their legal system and maintaining confidence in that is more important than an innocent man's life.

He'd made a good point. It is difficult to forget the shocking response by Prosecutor Dan Gershultz, which the court accepted, after Kenny's lawyer, Ken Parsigian, attempted to introduce the new forensic evidence that debunked Fire Marshal Cryer's theories – 'even though the new evidence may establish Richey's innocence, the Ohio and US constitutions nonetheless allow him to be executed because the prosecution did not know [at the time of the trial] that the scientific testimony offered at trial was false and unreliable.' Now my opinion may be biased but I'd say that any legal system that supports such thinking is inherently evil and sadistic.

Kenny was a tortured man, isolated in a concrete cell, kept alive for one purpose – to be killed by the State of Ohio. From afar, I felt my brother's pain. I too was mystified, unable to understand why the 6th Circuit were taking so long. Of course, I was unaware that, after a death sentence has been passed in Ohio, a reprieve is rarely granted. Ohio State records show that, from an estimated 2,500 appeals filed by nearly three hundred death row prisoners since 1981, only one led to a prisoner's freedom – one appeal out of 2,500. The odds were stacked against Kenny like a formidable prison wall. Maybe the 6th Circuit judges would change their minds and uphold Kenny's conviction? But I didn't believe it. I've never believed Ohio executioners would strap my brother into their electric chair or administer a lethal injection and take his life.

But, in a sense, I was wrong. I can't forget the face of the old man I saw being interviewed on the *American Justice* TV programme. What had happened to the brother I knew – the young, strong, healthy brother who had sometimes got me out of scrapes with older lads? They had taken him away and replaced him with a bitter old man. The hopes and dreams of the brother I knew *had* been murdered and nothing could bring them back. So, yes, in a sense, they had killed my brother. The only merciful thing for them to do was to allow him to have what remained of his life.

But October passed, followed by November and then December. Up until that time, I had been calling Dad once a week to find out if Kenny had received a decision from the 6th Circuit. As December passed into January 2005, my calls became less frequent. My growing convictions mirrored Kenny's own. Almost nine months had passed since the court questioned his conviction – nine months. Would there be any end soon? It didn't appear so.

On January the twenty-fifth, Kenny awoke and boiled the kettle for a cup of tea as he usually did. While he waited for the water to boil, he brushed his teeth and then washed his face. It was an abnormally sunny morning for January and he could feel its warmth as he looked through the narrow thick window. Heavy razor-wire fences encircled the cellblock but he was so used to seeing it he no longer noticed. It was Robert Burns Day – and my birthday. As he remembered that, he also remembered that he'd forgotten to send me a birthday card. Did it really matter? Birthdays no longer seemed important to either of us. July 2005, would mark his nineteenth year on death row. It's a long time for anyone to spend in prison, let alone on death row.

As he sat on his bunk and sipped his tea, a guard appeared at his cell door. He told Kenny that his lawyer had called and was waiting to talk to him. Kenny remembers a slight tremble in his hand as he set his cup down. An unscheduled call from Ken Parsigian could mean only one thing – a court decision had been rendered. Kenny took his time moving to his cell door to be shackled and cuffed. He took his time because he'd taken many of these journeys before where guards escorted him in chains to a room with a private telephone line for attorneys' calls. These journeys always ended in crushing disappointment, each taking a piece of his hopes.

After the guards led him to the room and fastened his ankle shackles to a D-ring on the floor, they left him alone. Only then did he lift the phone and press it to his ear. As Ken Parsigian talked, Kenny stared at the whitewashed cinderblock wall, dazed. He repeated his lawyer's first words over and over in his mind. 'In a two to one decision, the 6th Circuit have ruled to overturn your conviction. Ohio State must release you or retry you within ninety days . . .'

You might have expected Kenny to rejoice in a flood of emotions that had been held in check for almost nineteen years. He didn't. It was something that troubled him. Later, he sat at his desk in his cell and wrote to me about his subdued reaction:

> It's brilliant news, Tom. They have ninety days to retry me or let me go. I just wish I felt more excited about it. I should be dancing like a twit and jumping for joy but I'm not and I don't understand it at all. I could not have hoped for a better decision yet my feelings don't reflect that.
>
> What have they done to me? Maybe it all just hasn't sunk in yet or maybe I'm waiting until I actually walk out the front gate? I don't know. Maybe I've felt empty and dead inside for so long that I no longer have the ability to feel total joy and happiness? I'm happy about the decision, Tom, don't get me wrong. It's great. I'm going home. But I should feel happier than I do.

The 6th Circuit Court's decision exploded like an atomic bomb in Ohio. Across the Atlantic, while Kenny's supporters partied, the British media felt its impact and began calling the prison to request interviews. The general excitement was not shared by opponents of Kenny's release in Ohio State.

The office of Jim Petro, the Ohio Attorney General, posted a brief statement on its website, saying it was 'disappointed' by the judgement of the federal judges. Petro's chief spokesperson, Kim Norris, told the *Sunday Herald* that, despite the decision, they still believed Kenny is a murderer. 'The evidence still shows his guilt,' she said. 'Keep in mind that this is not the individual Attorney General's view. This is a case that was tried and has been reviewed by a number of courts in the United States. All of these courts, the Ohio Court of Appeals, the Ohio Supreme Court, the Federal District Court, have agreed that the evidence against Kenny Richey proved his guilt in committing this terrible crime. The evidence doesn't change.' Norris then threatened, 'There is a misconception that inmates who have their convictions and sentences overturned automatically go free. Well, they don't necessarily end up back on the street.'

Sour grapes?

The fact is that two of the three judges who reviewed Kenny's case slammed the integrity of the conviction. The court focused primarily on the incompetence of Kenny's trial lawyer, William Kluge, and his hiring of Gregory Dubois, the so-called forensic expert, who ended up testifying for the State. As it turned out, Dubois, who had only attended a couple of two-day courses on arson-related training, had been hired by Kluge through a flier he received in the mail. The court highlighted the deficiency of this 'expert' and other failings of William Kluge, stating that 'Counsel [Kluge] adopted a defence that rendered Richey a sitting duck.' The court further went on to state:

> Had counsel made the effort to find a qualified expert, rather than blindly hiring Dubois, the expert would have had the expertise and wherewithal to undermine the State's evidence that the fire was caused by arson. The record indicates that a competent arson expert would have all but demolished the

State's scientific evidence and, with it, a large part of the case against Richey.

The 6th Circuit even took the step of criticising its younger brother, the Federal District Court of Ohio, who had rejected Kenny's previous appeal. In defence of the State's forensic conclusions, the District Court had cited an article written by forensic scientist, Tony Cafe. However, upon learning this, Cafe subsequently declared that the District Court 'miscited and misunderstood my published articles' and that 'most of the world's leading forensic scientists in this field would be horrified if they saw the chromatograms used to convict Kenny Richey.' Cafe warned that if 'Kenny Richey were executed on the basis of this scientific evidence, then these chromatograms will become historical documents examined by scientists all over the world and used to show just how wrong forensic evidence can be'.

The court also attacked Kenny's conviction for aggravated felony murder. The court determined that, in order to convict a person for this crime, intent to kill the person who died must be proven. Even the State had admitted that Kenny had no intent to kill Cynthia Collins. This fact and the incompetence of William Kluge 'undermine [the State's] confidence in the reliability of Richey's conviction and sentence'.

Ohio authorities vowed to appeal the decision. Under federal procedural law, a party has fourteen days to request a full court review from the twelve 6th Circuit judges but such reviews are rarely granted, with some 400 requests made each year and only around ten cases accepted. The deadline for the State to request a review would be up at 5 p.m. on February the eighth.

Kenny and his lawyers expected the State would meet that deadline and file what is sometimes known as a 'spite appeal'. The only real purpose of it would be to prolong Kenny's stay on death row. Speaking to the Ohio *Lima News*, Kenny admitted that he held no hope that the State would drop the case. 'That would be the equivalent of admitting they were wrong and would open the gate for a lawsuit.' Ken Parsigian agreed that State prosecutors would probably seek a rehearing and added, 'Even if we have to go forward, even if it's not over, at least we're in the lead now. It's a lot better to go forward in the lead.'

In the days following the 6th Circuit decision, a reporter from the *Brainerd Dispatch* in Minnesota visited the town of Baxter, calling on a nineteen-year-old by the name of Sean. Kenny had no idea his son lived in Baxter, Minnesota. He had written to his son several times over the years but his letters were always sent back to him marked 'return to sender – addressee gone away'. Kenny's ex-wife, Wendy, had shielded Sean from Kenny. During his interview with the *Dispatch* reporter, Sean admitted knowing few details about his father. At around the age of ten, Wendy had told him that Kenny was in prison for killing a girl in a fire.

For the first time, Sean learned of some of the details of his father's case and the numbers of supporters amongst whom were some famous names. 'I didn't know how big this case was,' Sean said. 'Susan Sarandon and all of these celebrities and the Pope? Oh my God! This is nuts. It isn't something that happens everyday.' Told of the report by *The Scotsman* that quoted Kenny as saying he planned to track Sean down after his release, Sean admitted he'd like that. 'I want to see him too.'

On February the second, while being interviewed by *Good Morning TV*, Kenny was shown a picture of his nineteen-year-old son. He hadn't seen since the boy since he was a baby and he broke down. No doubt, Kenny has a lot of catching up to do but it may be a while before he can begin. Five days later, on February the seventh, the Ohio Attorney General's office filed a motion to extend the time to allow them the opportunity to prepare a petition for rehearing the 6th Circuit's decision. The court customarily grants such motions and did so in this case.

It extended the deadline for the State to appeal to February the twenty-second. However, the court warned that, after this one, no further extensions would be granted.

At the time of writing, Ohio Attorney General Petro has filed his petition, requesting the 6th Circuit for a rehearing. It is unlikely it will be granted. The next step for the Ohio authorities will be a Writ of Certiorari to the United States Supreme Court but this too is doomed to fail. America's highest court receives around 5,000 Writs of Certiorari a year and it usually only grants review for around eighty from that number. It selects the cases that will have far-reaching consequences for others across the country. For example, a woman's right to an abortion was established in the 1970s landmark case *Roe v Wade*, and recently, in *Blakely v Washington*, the US Supreme Court ruled that Washington State's procedure for imposing an exceptional sentence on kidnapper Ralph Blakely was unlawful. This ruling has breathed new hope into the lives of tens of thousands of prisoners across the United States who received exceptional sentences. Indeed, it is a decision which may secure my own release. Kenny's case has no such issues which could potentially affect hundreds of people so the US Supreme Court will deny Ohio's Writ of Certiorari.

In the meantime, the new Putnam County Prosecutor, Gary Lammers, stated that he plans to begin preparing for possible retrial. This would be Ohio's next option following denial by the US Supreme Court. The process will take longer than ninety days and Kenny understands that his time on death row may still be extended for many months. He doesn't care. He welcomes the prospect of a retrial. 'I want to go to retrial,' he said. 'Then I can walk free because we have the evidence that proves my innocence.'

In truth, a retrial is unlikely. The case is almost two decades old. Witnesses have dispersed, died and forgotten aspects of the case. More importantly, the forensic evidence heavily favours

Kenny's innocence. In all likelihood, the State of Ohio may offer Kenny another of its deals. In response to that prospect, Kenny has said, 'They probably will make an offer but I'm not taking it. Even if it was the only way for me to get out, I wouldn't take it. They've offered deals before and they can offer one now but bargaining is off. No plea bargains, no deals, nothing. It's a matter of honour.'

EPILOGUE

On April the nineteenth 2005, the 6th Circuit Court of Appeals denied the Ohio State's request for a rehearing *en banc* (a US legal term meaning 'by the full court') and they ordered Ohio authorities to release Kenny or retry him within ninety days.

Kenny's lawyer, Ken Parsigian, stated that there will be no retrial in Kenny's case for four reasons: Fire Marshal Cryer, now in his seventies, was diagnosed with Alzheimer's disease several years ago and he would not be an effective witness; Peggy Price changed her testimony, claiming, among other things, that she was pressured by the prosecution to admit that Kenny threatened to burn A-building; the state's 'scientific' testimony has been decimated; and the death penalty can never again be applied in Kenny's case. Because the aggravated murder count was thrown out, the state cannot bring this charge against Kenny again. To do so would amount to double jeopardy (being tried for the same crime twice), which is unlawful.

Ken Parsigian did say that the state could retry Kenny on the arson charge that Kenny was convicted of 'but their scientific evidence has been destroyed, plus Kenny has been in jail for nineteen years. How much time are you going to get?' He also stated, 'Twelve years ago I asked Kenny what he missed the most.' He said, "The first thing I want is a good Scottish beer." So I told him last week, "When they let you out, I will be standing there with two cold bottles of McEwans – one for you and one for me." I'll be there.'

It is expected that the State of Ohio will continue their spiteful process of continuing Kenny's confinement by filing a futile appeal to the US Supreme Court. They have ninety days in which to file. If they do file and the US Supreme Court denies the review, as is likely, Kenny anticipates finally getting to drink his cold McEwan's lager before the year is out.

EPILOGUE UPDATE

In the weeks following the 6th Circuit Court's denial of the Ohio Attorney General's request for a rehearing *en banc*, the Attorney General's office filed a motion to postpone the running of the ninety days until after their appeal to the US Supreme Court has been decided. Ken Parsigian did not delay in opposing the motion and, in his response, requested a mandate from the court ordering that the ninety-day countdown begin immediately.

On May the thirteenth 2005, Kenny received news that the 6th Circuit Court had reached a decision. It issued a mandate, ordering the State of Ohio to retry Kenny or release him within ninety days. The mandate was cause for a collective sigh from my family. A dream had started to become reality. On hearing the news, Mum cried and I've never heard Dad's voice sound so young and giddy.

Yet, May also carried whispers of concern. The prison doctor warned Kenny that he has an enlarged heart. I had to grit my teeth at the news. Apnea, diabetes and now an enlarged heart. While a part of me celebrates the possible vindication and perhaps the imminent freedom of my brother, another part of me mourns for the nineteen years on death row that has killed him.

Inexplicably, during the last week of May 2005, Kenny learned that the mandate that ordered the ninety-day countdown would not effectively begin until all twelve judges had signed the order. In practice, a mandate is usually signed by all presiding judges on the same day and it rarely takes more than a few days. The one judge withholding her signature is the sole judge who ruled against Kenny in the two-to-one decision of the 6th Circuit Court to overturn his conviction.

In theory, this judge could let the mandate lie untouched in her desk drawer for six months or more and delay Kenny's release. At the time of writing, on May the twenty-sixth, Ken Parsigian is preparing a motion to compel the mandate, with or without the malicious judges's signature.

'It's a typical example of what I've had to put up with all these years,' Kenny said. 'If I win my freedom, it will be after a long hard fight that's nearly seen the death of me. Now this judge wants to further torment me by prolonging my time on death row. Is that justice? It's Ohio justice.'

Despite stonewalling by the judge, Kenny remains confident he will bring in the New Year of 2006 in Scotland.

ADDENDUM

On May the third 2005, the remaining judge signed the mandate and the ninety-day countdown came in to effect. This meant that the Ohio authorities had until September the first to release Kenny or retry him. On June the thirtieth, the nineteenth anniversary of the fire that took young Cynthia's life, the new Putnam County Prosecutor, Gary Lammers, held a news conference and announced that it was his intention to retry Kenny.

Kenny didn't expect this outcome but it is actually what he has always wanted – the chance to prove his innocence and clear his name.